GOD'S RAVENS
STILL FLY

Ronnie McCracken

AMBASSADOR
Belfast • Greenville

God's Ravens Still Fly
© 1996 Ronnie McCracken

First published 1996

ISBN 1 - 898787 78 6

Cover photos by Author
St. Basils, Moscow.
Milk and Poultry on sale in the streets.

AMBASSADOR PRODUCTIONS LTD,
Providence House
16 Hillview Avenue,
Belfast, BT5 6JR

Emerald House,
1 Chick Springs Road,
Greenville,
South Carolina 29609

Ronnie McCracken

GOD'S RAVENS STILL FLY

The collapse of the Soviet Union led to an Exodus of the Jews.
When the Iron gates opened to let them out they also opened to allow us in.

This is the story of faith's response to the great challenge of our time as we have gone to Russia with love.

Dedication

God's Ravens Still Fly' *is dedicated to the memory of Rachel Zlotnik*
(nee Pokrzywa) who, with her husband and two children was taken
from the ghetto of Lodz and murdered in Auschwitz during the
Holocaust. They never had a chance to be refugees. There was no one
there to help them then. It must never be so again.

Contents

Foreword

The hairy figure sat hunched by the trickle that had once been a pleasant stream while the sun beat relentlessly down. Every day it had been the same, ever since he had gone to preach to Ahab and declared God's judgement on Israel's sin. The word of the Lord had come so clearly to him and he faithfully declared it, "There shall be no rain on the earth." So for these last nine hundred days and more the land had known no rain. At first it had seemed quite pleasant as every day the sun shone down, but gradually the land grew drier and drier. Ancient wells never known to fail even in the hottest summer eventually ran dry. In the second season crops started to fail and as things got worse cattle began to die. Now things were really bad all over the land and the only word that could be used to describe the situation was desolation. Even in the royal palace in Samaria the king and queen felt the effects of the drought and Ahab grew more angry every day. Search parties were sent out to look for Elijah the Tishbite with orders to apprehend him and bring him to Samaria. Ahab felt sure that if Elijah could be found and killed then things would return to normal. Search as they would they could not find the prophet, for God had hidden him at the brook Cherith to wait out the worst of the famine with a promise that he would be taken care of. The Lord had chosen to take care of his servant in a very remarkable way.

The Bible records it like this, "I have commanded the ravens that they feed thee there." Theologians have debated among themselves about whether or not it really was the ravens that fed him or if it could have been the Bedouin tribesmen. I am quite happy to stick with the ravens and find no difficulty in believing that every day God sent his feathered messengers to do His Divine bidding. Constantly they came on their daily calls, every morning and evening with bread and flesh to meet the practical needs of God's servant. Is it not remarkable that they did not devour the food themselves? Everywhere there was famine and hunger and death as the terrible drought took its toll. I am sure that they could have used the food themselves. Other starving predators could have attacked them on their journeys in their quest for sustenance. In spite of everything they came and kept on coming even when things got really desperate and birds fell dead out of a scorching sky. The days that Elijah spent at Cherith were remarkable days indeed, they were days when he proved that God's 'ravens' really did fly. When eventually even the brook Cherith failed and the time came when bread and flesh could no longer sustain God's servant. When it was obvious that without a supply of fresh water he would quickly succumb to the drought and die. When, even for Elijah all seemed lost, the Lord had already made provision for His servant in the home of a poor widow at Zarephath.

Elijah the Tishbite must be one of the most wonderful characters in the Bible and his time at Cherith is an inspiration to us all.

Later on at the great Carmel contest he experienced a wonderful victory when God sent fire from heaven. The hymn writer has summed it up like this, "Elijah's God still lives today." Not only is Elijah's God still living but His 'ravens' still fly. They might not come as the feathered creatures did to Cherith long ago but He still has His 'ravens' and they appear just when they are needed, they come in unexpected ways and they differ in appearance. Sometimes they wear hats and coats and gloves in this modern age instead of feathers. Sometimes we know who they are and sometimes we have no idea who they are or where they have come from. One incontrovertible fact remains the same, whatever the circumstances, whatever the needs, whatever the challenge, for those who trust Him.

God's ravens still fly

CHAPTER ONE

"Let My People Go"

The telephone rang; its shrill tones compelling my attention. I answered with the familiar, "01232-825419, Who is calling please?" having little idea of what was about to take place or of what was going to happen during the next few weeks. The caller asked if I had seen a television programme the previous night about Russian Jews who were stranded in Italy. It is very seldom that I am at home on any evening and I was not even aware that there had been such a programme. However my interest was stirred and further enquiries revealed that the programme was called "First Tuesday." It had been a documentary presented by Olivia O'Leary about Russian Jews who were being refused permission to travel on to America. The programme was entitled, "Uncle Sam's Refuseniks" and depicted the plight of Soviet Jews who had been refused entry visas for the United States. A change in US Government policy had left these people stranded in Italy.

Next morning I decided to telephone to the television company and asked if there was any way they could let me have a copy of the video tape of the programme. I spoke to a girl called Jane and after some minutes she explained that it would not be possible for her to let me have a copy of the tape.

There would be many difficulties concerning getting authorisation to make a copy, permission would be needed from many different sources that would take time and it could be expensive. As we spoke a bit more I tried to persuade her and explained that I really wanted very much to see this programme and that I was so disappointed not to have seen it. At last she agreed to let me have a copy from the archives if I would promise to return it promptly afterwards. The lady explained that she would get into big trouble if I did not return the tape, it was more than her job was worth. I faithfully promised that as soon as I would look at the programme I would send the tape straight back to her. I can remember saying to my wife after that telephone conversation, "I am sure that lady will not bother to send the tape for she does not know me." However the lady kept her word and posted the tape to me and a few days later it arrived at our home where it was to make a tremendous impact. I have no doubt that at the time Jane did not know she was one of God's 'ravens', certainly I didn't.

The Lord was using her to help set in motion a great work that was to have very far reaching consequences. I had no idea that the conversation with Jane and her response in sending the tape to me was going to have such an influence.

Had I been able to visualise in advance all that was to come I am sure that my faith would have failed and doubt would have paralysed my ability to trust in the Lord. How very wonderful is the Lord our God in that He only lets us see a little at a time lest we should be overcome by our fears.

If some person had told me at the beginning of January 1990 that we would be involved in delivering thousands of copies of the Bible to Russian Jews before Easter it would have seemed like an impossible dream. If someone had told me that I would preach the Gospel to hundreds of Soviet Jews at one time I could not have believed it possible. If someone had predicted that we would turn our house into a warehouse for food, blankets, sweets and thousands of pieces of Christian literature in Russian, I think we would have thought them crazy.

"God's Ravens Still Fly" is the account of how all these and subsequent miraculous events took place. It is the true story of how the Lord provided for every need. The arrival of that video tape set in motion a chain of events that is still going on and that reaches across the continents. I am grateful to Jane that she kept her word and sent on the tape to us. I am grateful to Thames Television who made it available without cost and even paid the postage! When the Lord is in something then every detail falls into place and He causes His 'ravens' to fly.

When the tape finally arrived at my home I made arrangements with Mr. George McConnell to come to my home with the necessary equipment so that we could view the tape. George is the son of Joel and Rae who are known all over Ireland for their beautiful duet singing. As I did not have the means to view the tape George agreed to bring his equipment to my home one evening.

I invited a few friends to come to the house that night to watch the tape and as it was being shown I was looking through tear misted eyes. There was such a longing in my heart for those dear Soviet Jewish people. I was just full of longing to get out there to Italy to be among them and to try to share the Gospel with the Lord's ancient people. One big problem for me was the fact that I had just returned home after spending five weeks preaching in churches and witnessing to Jews in South Africa, how could I say to my wife, "Pat, I think I will go off again to Italy." I thought I had better say nothing and just keep my longing sealed up in my heart. Pat had heard something about the situation from me and now as the video tape ended and even before the machine was switched off she turned to me and said, "I think you should get out there to Italy as soon as possible. I had better start packing your things for you." I really wanted to go but I felt that I could not just set off on my own initiative or go just because I was feeling moved from watching the video. The Lord would have to give me clear instructions so that I would know that it was His will. I had many meetings arranged and could not easily change them. People were depending on me to turn up and some of those meetings had been arranged for a very long time. I went to the study and got down before the Lord to ask His will concerning the matter.

I spent some time speaking to the Lord in prayer after which I turned to the Word of the Lord for guidance about what I should do. As I read from the Bible the Lord spoke to me out of Ecclesiastes chapter seven and verse eighteen. "It is good that thou shouldest take hold of this, yea also from this withdraw not thine hand......" The Lord spoke so clearly that I could not doubt it then or at any time since. Take hold of this and do not withdraw your hand. This is the text God gave me and which He has held me to ever since. I was left with no alternative but to go forward at His direction.

From the beginning it was the Lord who arranged and who did this work. He did it all. Not for the glory of any man but for His own glory and for the glory of His people Israel. We were but the instruments to whom He gave the privilege to share in a small part of His great plan. At first I was reluctant to tell this story but several friends pressed me saying "The story must be told to glorify the Lord." I began to write and after many months of hard work the text was complete. All was edited and corrected and the final draft was on the computer ready for the printer. At just that critical moment my house was broken into and the study ransacked. Two computers were stolen and along with all our office records we lost, "God's Ravens Still Fly." It was a devastating blow and I thought afterwards that the book would never be published, only now have I been able to try to restore what was stolen. Only now have I been able to find the time to set down in print once more the amazing story of answered prayer and Divine provision. Only now has it been possible for me to find the courage to replace the work that was stolen. Some well meaning friends told me that the Lord arranged for it to be stolen because He did not want it to be published. I realised how wrong they were when I remembered that those who break through and steal are not the servants of the Lord but of the devil.

 . The Lord has done great things and I tell the story here that others might realise that, God's ravens' still fly.

CHAPTER TWO

A Chinese Connection

What on earth could the Chinese have to do with Russian Jewish refugees in Italy? It certainly seems like a mystery wrapped in an enigma. The answer however is really very simple. When the Lord is in control He works out His purposes in His own wonderful ways. For very many years I have also been interested in the Chinese people and their spiritual needs. It was my greatest desire in my youth to be a missionary in China but of course Chairman Mao did not want foreign missionaries. One day I discovered that there were Chinese people all over the world as well as in China, they were even in Belfast! I contacted the Chinese Overseas Christian Mission in London and asked its director Mary Wang to send me a team of Chinese evangelists to reach the people who had come to live in Ireland. After some initial hesitation Mary sent me a team of young people led by Nai Bn Cham. They faithfully visited the restaurants and the students and as a result of their efforts a Belfast Chinese Christian Fellowship was formed. This was soon followed by Dublin Chinese Christian Fellowship and then Coleraine and Jordanstown and Galway. The development of the work among the Chinese students led us to organise an annual Christmas conference for the young people.

For fourteen years I attended each conference to help the Chinese young people with all the arrangements. As the 1989/90 Christmas New

Year period approached we were looking forward to the conference that was to be held at Avoca Manor, the Scripture Union house in the Irish Republic. The speaker was to be Pastor Frank Cheung from Birmingham, an outstanding Chinese Christian who has a great ministry to the restaurant workers. On many previous occasions Frank and I had enjoyed rich fellowship and lots of laughs together.

During the conference Frank and I were having a chat one day and he asked me what I was involved in specifically for the Lord just then. I began to tell him about the Jews from Russia being in Italy and he said to me, "You must go at once. I have a friend in Rome who owns a Chinese restaurant and I will phone to him and ask him if he will look after you when you get there." As soon as Frank arrived back home in Birmingham he telephoned to Rome and made all the arrangements. This was just another of the many miracles we experienced during those days. Frank Cheung was another of the Lord's 'ravens' sent to supply a need and to make a way where there was no way.

Frank's friend is called Mr. Wong and he is the owner of a restaurant in the centre of Rome called, 'LA PACE.' Mr. Wong is also a leader of the Chinese community in Italy and a bright Christian.

A few days after Frank had returned to his home I received a message that Mr. Wong would meet me at the airport in Rome on my arrival and guide me to his shop in the city centre. That all sounded very good to me but there was one major problem, Mr. Wong did not speak a word of English! I could speak neither Italian nor Chinese and the thought of a Chinese speaking Italian directing an Ulsterman driving a hire car through Rome's chaotic traffic was just too much! As the time drew near for me to fly to Rome I asked one of our Chinese young people to make a telephone call for me to tell Mr. Wong not to meet me at the airport. Somehow I would make my own way to his shop in Rome.

The problem now was that Mr. Wong spoke only the Shanghai dialect and my friend spoke Cantonese with a Belfast accent! In the course of translation the message got a bit confused and somehow I ended up with the wrong address in Rome. Of course as I boarded the flight on January 13 I did not know that, and I did not know what to expect on my arrival. I had no idea where I would be staying that first night in Italy. I could not have imagined that I would be making many journeys there within the next few weeks or that I would be transporting thousands of Russian Bibles and tens of thousands of pounds worth of materials to Italy.

I had no idea that I would soon be scouring Europe for Christian literature in Russian. Surely it is just as well that the Lord in His wisdom conceals some things from us, for faith would waver and perhaps fail if we could see all the challenge at one time.

On my arrival at Fiumicino airport I collected my luggage and located my rented car and set off into Rome to look for the 'La Pace' Chinese Restaurant. I had never before been in Rome and had no idea where I was going. The staff at the car rental desk pointed me towards the airport exit and I set off into the Saturday evening traffic. Driving in Italy was a new experience and I dared not look around me to see where I was going but just followed the traffic in front. Everyone appeared to be in a tremendous hurry and the traffic seemed to be racing along the autostrada in a way that would strike terror into faint hearts. After driving for quite some time in the general direction of Rome I began to enter the city, the Saturday evening traffic was unbelievable. When I thought it was time to ask for directions I drew up next to a man to make enquiries. "Do you speak English?" I yelled over the roar of the traffic. He replied, "A little, a very little." I asked him for a street called "Via Dimante" which was the name I had been given and which was written on my piece of paper. The man looked at me and said, "That is not the street you want." He went to his car and came back with a map and a street directory and looked for the correct name. This turned out to be, Via Della Madonna Diamante.

I think that without his help I would have been searching for a long time for a street that did not exist. He was a great help to me and was just another 'raven' the Lord sent along in time of need. After a lot of frantic arm waving and some words of English interspersed with Italian I was off again. Soon I came to the Coliseum where in ancient times so many Christians met their death as martyrs for their faith. I did not dare to look about too much for the traffic was hurtling around that magnificent ruin in a fashion that no charioteer could ever have dreamt of in the old days.

Thinking that I must be near the street where the 'La Pace' was located I asked a policeman for help. "You cannot go there by car, you must go by your feet," he said. Finding a parking place was going to be a problem so I asked him where I could park. "Park here," he said gesturing towards what looked remarkably like a no parking sign. When I protested that it was a no parking area he said, "This is Italy my friend, we have many laws here but nobody keeps them." That may have been an overstatement but the more I drove in Italy the more convinced I became that it was not far off the mark.

When I had parked the car I walked for a few hundred yards through some small streets to Via Della Madonna Diamante. There I found the 'La Pace' restaurant where I met Mr. Wong. With typical Chinese hospitality he insisted on feeding me and soon a very large dish of non kosher food was set before me. All kinds of shellfish were there, cockles, mussels, limpets, clams and all manner of other creatures from the sea. I am mildly allergic to such creatures and so I ate with less enthusiasm than the others around the table. It was really very kind of Mr. Wong to offer to feed me and such things are a delicacy to the Chinese but as they swallowed the shellfish and spat out the shells it was a big struggle for me. I was happy when the meal was finally finished. Afterwards Mr. Wong wanted to take me to the airport. I don't think it was because I did not like his food! He seemed to think I was about to leave Rome and did not understand that I had just arrived! It took a lot of sign language to convince him that I was not on my way back to Ireland but at last he understood.

Once he got the message he signalled to me that I should go with him and getting into his car we set off through Rome at breakneck speed. Our first call was at a coffee shop where we drank a small cup of coffee. He downed his in one gulp but I had to sip mine slowly for it seemed to my yet unadapted palate that it was strong enough to keep one awake for about a week! Later I came to really enjoy Italian coffee. On leaving the coffee shop we went next door and climbed a flight of stairs, pointing at a closed door he indicated by gesturing at his watch that I should come back here next morning at 10.30 am. I realised that it was a church and that there would be a service next morning.

Mr. Wong then took me to a hotel and insisted on paying for my room for two nights. How very kind and generous this good man was to a stranger who could not even say thank-you to him properly.

Mr. Wong was another of the many 'ravens' the Lord sent along to help me on my way. A Chinese man who could not utter one word of my language and whose native tongue it is impossible for me to understand. What a privilege it has been to meet such people, the saints of the Lord from every background. After a good rest in a comfortable hotel room I was ready next morning when another Chinese man came to lead me to the church. He was able to speak a few words of English but we still had quite some fun trying to understand each other as we walked through Rome. We seemed to walk a long way before we reached the church and long before we arrived I was wishing that we had taken my car. When at last we did enter the church I was delighted to find that it was crowded with people. In fact all the seats were occupied and some members of the congregation were standing around the walls. I was offered a seat that some other friend had kindly vacated for me and I gratefully sat down. The service proceeded in a fairly normal kind of way with hymns and prayers and preaching of the Word. Then the Pastor announced that he was going to baptise some new converts and while he was preparing for that a Philippino man came to the pulpit. He made some announcements and then he asked in English if there were any visitors attending the church that day for the first time. Since I was a visitor I raised my hand along with several other people.

This dear man then spoke to me directly from the pulpit and asked me who I was and where I was from. I replied by saying that I was sort of a Pastor from Northern Ireland who had a special interest in the Jews. I was given a warm welcome by this man who said that he knew that many people came from Ireland to visit the Vatican but that I was the first one he had seen at the Evangelical Church!

As he welcomed me from the pulpit he said, "If you are interested in the Jews you should contact Pastor Joel, he works with the Russian Jewish refugees." As soon as the service ended I went up to the Philippino man and after a few more words of explanation he gave me Pastor Joel's address and telephone number. This proved to be the Lord's direction for me. My Philippino brother was one of the Lord's 'ravens' that day without even knowing about it. He put me in touch with Pastor Joel and that resulted in the wonderful things that followed. If he had not been there that day or if had he not spoken as he did I might never have met Joel and become involved in the work that he was doing among the Soviet Jews. I could easily have looked around for a few days at the sights of Rome and not have found the Russian Jews at all.

I would not have known exactly where to look or at which time to be in a certain place. It was the Lord who sent me at His bidding and He had His 'ravens' all along the way to meet the need at every point.

On my return from the church Mr. Wong had some more Chinese food ready for me and this time it was more to my taste. It was during that lunch that something wonderful happened which only the Lord could have arranged. Some days previously a Chinese woman had arrived in Italy illegally. Originally from Mainland China she was studying in England and was due to return home when the massacre took place in Tien An Mein square in Beijing. Although her British visa was running out she did not want to return to China and had been told by a friend that she might be allowed to stay in Italy. Cha Ling had made the trip to Rome using the last of her money in hope of getting a visa. Almost destitute she had gone into a shop in Rome to look around and there she met Mr. Wong. On hearing her sad story this good man arranged a job for her as a nanny and was trying to find a way to help her. Since Cha Ling could speak English she was now pressed into service to act as an interpreter for me. As we sat eating lunch she explained that I was to go to the Chinese church that afternoon where I would preach and she would try to interpret for me. I did not want the expected speaker to be set aside so we made an agreement that he would preach as arranged and I would just give a short address at the end. How happy I was that afternoon in Rome to see so many Chinese gathered in the name of the Lord Jesus and praising His name. Cha Ling had not been exposed to the Gospel message before and was very interested in the messages. After the service at the Chinese church was finished we went to several different places in Rome to visit Chinese families. I spoke to them about the situation for the Christians and the Church in China. I showed them some photographs that I had taken with my dear old friend the late Pastor Wang Ming Tao shortly after his release from prison. This valiant Chinese pastor had spent twenty-two years in prison for his refusal to deny the Lord. Jing Wun, his wife, served nineteen years in a forced labour camp. It had been my privilege to visit them in their home in Shanghai after they were freed and reunited. We spoke of how the Lord had sustained them through all their trials and of how He was still keeping them. The pastor had become almost completely deaf and Jing Wun was blind as a result of their many sufferings in prison.

The Chinese Christians were very interested to hear all about my experiences in China during an earlier visit when Chairman Mao had ordered the Great Proletarian Cultural Revolution. Cha Ling was also deeply interested in all we were saying. We spoke about the Baptismal service we had witnessed that morning at the church.

All these conversations had to be interpreted by Cha Ling so she had a busy time, doing a lot of talking and all the time hearing about the Lord. That evening when we returned to Mr. Wong's, Cha Ling asked me if I would be willing to help her with some English pronunciation that she was finding difficulty with. I readily agreed but warned her that she might end up with a Belfast accent if she followed my pronunciation. As she sat there with her English dictionary in her hand I asked her to pronounce the words Christ, Christian and Christianity. Chinese people often have difficulty with the R sounds which tend to come out as L. Over and over again Cha Ling repeated the sounds as she tried to master the English pronunciation. I asked her if she knew who Christ was and she replied, "Is it a person, is it someone?" I began to tell her very simply the story of Jesus, about His birth and life. I told her about how He loves us and wants to forgive us all our sins. I spoke about how He preached and fed the hungry, about how He healed the sick and the afflicted and about all His wonderful works. Then I explained how when He was thirty-three years old His own people had rejected Him and demanded that He be put to death. As I was describing to her the crucifixion and death of our Saviour she looked at me in amazement and said, "Just when the story was getting good why did you have to go and spoil it." As we continued our conversation I explained that this was not the end of the story, Jesus had really died for us and it is through His death that we can have the gift of eternal life. I used a very simple illustration to explain what I was trying to say, it was just like her visa problem. There was a place which she absolutely did not want to go to, China. There was a place which she did very much want to go to and where she would like to stay, England. The problem was that in order to stay in England she needed permission from the authorities and the difficulty was how to get permission to live in the Queen's realm. In just the same way there are two places where our soul can go for eternity. One is called Hell and is a very bad place to go, at all costs we must avoid it. The other is called Heaven and there everything is perfect and glorious; and where for all eternity those who love God will be happy and blest. To go there we need permission from the authority, its sort of like getting a visa.

The only one who can give us that visa is the Lord Jesus. He gave His life in order to have the right to give Eternal Life to all those who trust in Him. Whoever believes in Jesus will never be thrown out of Heaven or asked to leave for they will have the right to be permanent residents in the land which He is preparing for His followers. Not only did He die for us' on the cross at Calvary but He rose again from the tomb and He is alive for ever more.

Cha Ling sat back in her chair and asked me, "Can it be true? Can it really be so?" I assured her that it was really true and that this is the essence of the Gospel.

As she digested this new message she said to me, "I think I will change my mind and believe in God." Cha Ling indicated that she would like to read more about this good news in 'The Book' so that she could really understand it.

Then she added, "Maybe when I do believe, maybe one day I will come to Ireland and you could wash me in the tank." I had to smile at her expression. The word baptism was not yet in her vocabulary. It was about five weeks later that I received a welcome letter from Cha Ling telling me that she had indeed decided to become a Believer.

As we sat talking about these things in Mr. Wong's I could not help relfecting that maybe the Lord had a completely different plan in bringing me to Italy than I had imagined. I had come in the interest of the Soviet Jews but here I was preaching to a lady from mainland China. May be this was all His plan in bringing me to Italy.

I told the Lord that it was all right with me if this was what He wanted and that even if I did not meet a single Jew from Russia I was glad to know that He was working out His own purposes in the life of Cha Ling. I couldn't know it at that moment but the Lord had much larger plans than I could even dream about, plans that He would unfold step by step and that would result in things I could not even imagine then.

CHAPTER THREE

On A Black Beach

Early on Monday morning I prepared to set off from Rome to try and find the Soviet Jews in the small town that had featured in the television documentary. As I prepared to check out of the hotel I asked the receptionist if it was very far to Ladispoli. He replied that it was about five minutes drive away! I knew that this could not be correct because it took longer than five minutes to get to the end of the street. A few more enquiries revealed that Ceiro, the receptionist, did not want to discourage hotel guests who asked for directions so his stock answer in English was always five minutes! Actually in the event it took me over an hour to get out of the parking place, some Roman driver had double parked and trapped me. I had to fetch the police with their car removing crane before I was able to proceed. In spite of the delay I was in good spirits as I set off to look for the way to the autostrada. The sun was shining brightly when I set out and as I drove along I was praying to the Lord. I was praying not just because of the chaotic and dangerous traffic, but because I was so happy to be on my way. I had such a peace in my heart as I felt the assurance that I was in the centre of His will. Although I was going to a place I had never been to before and where I knew absolutely no one, although I had no idea where I would sleep that night I did not feel at all anxious. It was just good to be moving in God's perfect plan. After a few false starts I eventually found my way to the autostrada and drove in the general direction that had been pointed out to me. About thirty-five minutes later I saw the first sign for Ladispoli and prepared to leave at the next exit. I had no idea what to expect of Ladispoli apart from the glimpses I had seen on the video tape. The town itself is small with a population of about ten thousand. It has a rather run down appearance and is mainly composed of apartment blocks. Many of these apartments are normally rented out to summer visitors who come to this town just to the North of Rome to escape the stifling heat of the city in summer. The beach is very unusual in that it is black volcanic sand that is supposed to give off medicinal rays when heated by the sun. Lots of people come to Ladispoli just to lie on the sand to try and get some relief from their aches and pains. I imagine that it is quite a pleasant spot in the summer time and no doubt the holiday makers really enjoy themselves there. On this January day it looked a rather dismal and unattractive place. As I approached the square that the Italians call the Piazza I could see crowds of Soviet Jews milling around the centre and crowds more walking in the nearby park like avenue that I later learned the Russians called 'The Alley'. I quickly parked the car and walked back to take a closer look and to listen to the sound of the Russian voices.

One person was trying to give English lessons to a small group under a tree while not far away someone else was trying to sell a kind of deep fried dough the Russians call Borekas.

As I walked about among the people I was deeply moved as I saw so many trying to sell all kinds of things. Later on I came to understand that because the rouble was not a convertible currency the people had to leave with only the equivalent of ninety roubles. In order to try and bring something with them from their life's work in Russia they had used their roubles to buy as many Russian goods and souvenirs as they could carry with them in hopes that they would be able to sell them in Italy to obtain money for food and essentials. Even though they had been receiving very small salaries by western standards many had been able to save some money in Russia. A qualified doctor was then only earning around one hundred and twenty roubles each month which at the time was about twelve English pounds. Even with such small wages it was difficult to spend this amount in Russia as everything was in such short supply. These people had come from a country that was sadly in great difficulty economically. Many of the shops in Moscow and Leningrad had few goods to display.

So having saved up a quantity of roubles the Jews found that they could not take them out of the country and they could not exchange them for other currency. The only possibility was to buy Russian goods that they would then try to sell in order to get some ready cash. As most of the people were selling the same things and as all the Russian goods are of pretty poor quality there was a very competitive market. The Italians were buying some things but at poor prices. After observing for a time this pathetic scene I walked to the beach nearby, there too I found crowds of Russian Jews sitting in the semi-derelict changing rooms and shower cubicles as they sheltered from the chilling wind.

Some people were studying tattered English text books and some were writing letters while others just sat and gazed wistfully out to sea. As I turned to leave the black beach I marvelled at how a strange providence had taken these Jews from all over Russia and the former Soviet Union and brought them here to this place. Why to Italy? Why to Ladispoli? Why did the Lord bring them to this kind of non-place that seemed to me on that January day to be next door to nowhere?

While I was walking along and musing on these things I bumped into a young man and we began to talk together, he was the first Russian Jew I was able to speak to in Italy. Benjamin Shukman was a refugee from persecution and oppression. A talented young man and a qualified engineer, here he was in Ladispoli happy to have found a part time unofficial job stacking shelves in a shop. As he told me of his life in Russia and now in Italy and how he had been refused permission to go on to America as a refugee he sighed and said, "Life is not a bed of roses."

I discovered that the Jewish aid organisations were doing marvellous work in trying to help these people but that there was simply not enough money to meet all the needs. People were being supported while they were recognised as political refugees and receiving enough to pay for accommodation with a little left for food. When they applied for a visa to the United States, if they were refused, they then ceased to be supported. At one stage over five thousand people were stranded in Ladispoli in this kind of limbo situation as the American Government cracked down on visas to force more of the people to go to Israel. The very success of American foreign policy regarding the Jews from Russia had become an embarrassment to the United States. While governments waver and make secret deals and apply undeclared quotas it is as always the innocent people who suffer. I had been deeply moved by the story of one lady on the video tape documentary. I saw how she wept as she revealed that her apartment cost ninety thousand lira a month while she received only eighty thousand for an allowance. As she shed those bitter tears she had said, "How can I live, they will not let me go to America, I am afraid to go to Israel, will I have to return to Russia?"

When I returned to walk in the market place I quickly fell into conversation with some more of the Russian Jews. Most of them have a desire to go to America and to do this they need to learn English. Lots of people were eager to practice what they had been studying, the results were sometimes interesting grammatically. I began to speak with one man and as we stood looking at some rather mouldy and battered mandarin oranges I made the mistake of saying that I was not too impressed with the quality. I instantly regretted my thoughtless words when he turned on me angrily saying, "Where you come from this may be poor quality but where I have come from it is like paradise even to see them. When I was in Russia I could not find them and now that I am in Italy they might as well be in the museum for I cannot buy them".

As the daylight began to fade and darkness descended I needed to quickly find somewhere to sleep for the night, it proved to be impossible to find a hotel in Ladispoli. The one hotel that looked as if it might be functioning was closed for the winter season. I had to drive around for quite some time before l found a place called the El-Paso guest house, actually I found out afterwards that I was not very far from Ladispoli as I had made a big circle in my search. It proved to be a good location for me as about twenty minutes took me back to the main centre where the Russian Jews were standing around. Having established my base for the next few days I now set about making contact with Pastor Joel.

CHAPTER FOUR

Pastor Joel

After breakfast at the El Paso guest house I asked if I could use the telephone at the reception desk and eventually managed to make contact with Pastor Joel. I introduced myself and explained how I had obtained his telephone number. We chatted for a little while and I was aware that the American voice on the phone was less than enthusiastic about my call, he was being decidedly cagey and asking all kinds of penetrating questions. Rather than being put off by this approach I immediately formed the opinion that this was an excellent man and felt a bond of fellowship rising in my heart even before we met each other. When a little later we met at his centre to discuss things this initial feeling was confirmed and I was thrilled as I realised that God had brought us together in His perfect plan. We had never met before that day and had no knowledge of each other's existence but the Lord knew us both and we were in the Lord's hands.

Pastor Joel is the son of a pastor who had a great love for the Jews. The pastor and his wife, who were childless, promised God that if he would give them a son they would not only dedicate the boy to the Lord's service but they would dedicate him for work among the Jews. Eventually Joel was born and as he grew up it was often a frustration when people would pat him on the head and ask if he was going to be a preacher like his daddy. In the fullness of time the Lord met with Joel and saved him by His Grace and did indeed call him to full time work. At first he worked among American Indians but at last the Lord called him to the work among the Jews. I have no hesitation in saying that this man is a chosen vessel ordained to bring forth much fruit. Joel had been sent by his mission to Italy and was based in the Rome area. Although he was very faithful to his work there he was often frustrated because there were so few Jews in the area where he was working.

One day a man called at his house to ask if he would be interested in doing some evangelism among Russian Jews. Joel was not at home but his wife knew he would be excited at the prospect. The caller that day was a man who worked with The Messianic Testimony. Soon the two men were reaching out to the Jews from Russia who had begun to transit through Italy. At the first attempt to have an open air meeting the interpreter was the only convert! Then one day Joel woke up to the fact that there were ten thousand Soviet Jews in Ladispoli alone. From that moment he spared no effort to help the people and worked tirelessly to assist them in every way. Just at the very time when the biggest wave of Russian Jews was passing through Italy and just when Pastor Joel's resources where exhausted from trying to meet the needs of the people, the Lord sent me to Italy to help him. For me it has been a great honour to know Joel and his wife and to be permitted by the Lord to have the wonderful privilege to share a little with them in their work.

After we had talked a bit more and I shared something concerning my burden for the Jews he invited me to spend the next few days with him to see something of the work. We would go that very night to a nearby town to have a Bible study in an apartment with Jewish people and then go on to distribute literature at a place where the people congregate. That evening was for me a revelation and an experience that was to light a fire in my soul that would have consumed me had I not acted to do something to meet the needs which I saw. At the appointed hour we assembled beside a rather battered looking mini-bus and I was introduced to the other members of the evangelistic team. There was Sam, Pavel, Paul, Sergei and Sasha all Russian Jews who were coming to help distribute Gospel literature to their own people.

I think that was the first thing that made my heart catch fire, here were the fruits of Joel's labour of love sitting beside us. Also in the mini bus there was Vincent from New York, he had come for five weeks to assist in the outreach as the work was so large. With his bushy black beard he looked just like a Jew from Russia himself until he began to speak and then there could be no mistaking his origins. Vincent and I knew a lot of people who are involved in Jewish ministries both in the States and Israel so we had much to chat about. I still had the feeling that I was being vetted somewhat to determine just who and what I was, after all a strange person turning up unannounced from Northern Ireland could really be anyone.

Opponents of Gospel work among the Jews have been known to do all kinds of dirty tricks to get information and cause disruption and then there are lots of freaks around these days as well so one cannot be too careful.

After quite some time we arrived at the appointed place and began to carry in boxes containing study Bibles and other materials, some food was brought for needy families and some clothes and blankets. The interior of the apartment was sparse and cold but soon a number of Russian Jews gathered in and after a while Joel left to go to another place while Vincent commenced the Bible study from Mark's Gospel. The Bible study in Mark's Gospel that night was a wonderful experience for me, Vincent explained the Gospel to those Soviet Jews and answered all their questions that they fired at him, usually through the interpreter. The people also wanted to know all about the United States and life there right down to the cost of a ride on the underground.

Then one lady asked me a question about my experience with the Lord. I had been sitting quietly trying to refrain from speaking during the discussions. This is no easy feat for a preacher who is so often speaking but I did not want my new friends to think that I was trying to push myself into their work. Besides I had no experience as to how to approach these kind of Jews and I was afraid that I might say the wrong thing and hinder the work of the Lord. Evidently the lady noticed that this stranger was very silent and was curious about who he might be and what he believed. She may have been Russian and Jewish but the feminine instinct for information is universal. Since she asked I had no alternative but to begin to answer the question, so I began to speak with a glance at Vincent who nodded that it was all right to go ahead. In the middle of what I was saying the door opened and Pastor Joel arrived back to take us to the next place, if he was surprised to find me speaking he did not show it but I could see that he was listening very carefully to every word I said.

There was a very wonderful sense of the Lord Jesus present in that apartment and I felt sure that God was speaking to some of these dear people. After a few more moments we had to say our good-byes and return to the cold night air outside, it would have been nice to stay longer but time was pressing and we had some distance to go. I was really not prepared for what I witnessed next that evening for I had never seen anything like it before. To help you understand I had better explain that the people had to come to certain places for what they call 'The Posts'. A representative of the Jewish organisations came and called out the names of people from a list with instructions as to their situation. Some people would receive the good news that they were to leave for America, Canada or Australia and details were given to them about their report time for transport to the airport and so on. Incidentally they often had to report around three o'clock in the morn- ing for processing even though their flight might not be until eleven o'clock. Other people would receive the news that they must go to Rome to the office of the Hebrew Immigrant Aid Society or to see their case worker. The instruction to see a case worker usually seemed to mean a refusal by the American Government to grant them refugee sta- tus. You can understand that everyone had to attend the 'Post' to get the necessary information and every night some were very happy while others were very sad especially when families were divided.

Our next stop was to be the 'Post' at one of these areas to the North of Rome. The first thing that impressed me was the sheer number of people milling around, it actually felt a bit intimidating at first until I realised how gentle and gracious these people are. They are mainly highly educated and very well qualified individuals and almost with- out exception they received us with gratitude. It was so moving to see little families clinging together, the sad eyed children shyly holding on to mothers' skirts in the midst of the large crowd.

The night was really cold as we moved among the throng and the air was filled with vapour as the warm breath condensed in the atmosphere.

My heart cried out to the Lord for that promise to be fulfilled when He would breathe into them and they would become living souls. My cheeks were wet with tears as I marvelled at what God was doing in bringing them out from the North country at last. I had often read about this in the study at home and I had preached about it all over Northern Ireland and beyond, that was theory, this was reality. It is one thing to read about something and it is one thing to preach about it, but it is entirely something else to be standing in the middle of the throng and saying to yourself this is it. Pastor Joel instructed us to go out into the crowd two by two with the literature while he would remain at the van to speak to those individuals who would come to him.

I was delegated to go with Sam, so with a box of literature we two set off into the throng. Sam was a tall man dressed in a dark pin stripe suit with a nice white shirt but like most Russians without any tie. I had my heavy anorak on but still felt cold and my feet were freezing, I thought Sam must be perished with cold but he did not show any discomfort. Since Sam was a fairly recent believer I thought it would be best if he carried the box and I would distribute the literature as we moved among the crowd. In a very short time our box was empty and we returned to the van to find a lot of people crowded round the back doors talking to Joel and Vincent. I was just standing there watching when a man approached me and beckoned me to follow him to the front of the van, after a few moments he said to me, "Do you have the whole Bible? I heard that there is a whole Bible not just the new part. I would like a whole Bible to read about my ancestors."

Just before I had left my home I picked up eight copies of the Bible in Russian that had been on my bookshelf for quite some time. I had thought to myself they might come in handy if I met some Russian speakers and I had them in my shoulder bag that night. As I had seen the eager way in which the people were grabbing for the New Testament I realised that if they thought I had the whole Bible there would be a rush. So I said to this man, "Look if I give you one you must promise me that you will not tell any one I gave it to you." He duly promised and I slipped him a Bible that he quickly put under his coat. I think I will never forget that Russian Jew standing there stroking the bulge on his jacket and saying, "All of my life I have dreamed to see a Bible." In a very short time my other seven Bibles were gone and I was wishing that I had been able to bring many more.

It was after eleven o'clock that night when we began our return journey to Ladispoli. We were a tired but rejoicing band and I could not speak when Joel said to me, "Well Ronnie, what do you think about the work, is it not wonderful work?" Wonderful seemed an understatement.

I have laboured among Jews in Ireland and Israel, in Poland, South Africa and Gibraltar. I have spoken to Jews in Hong Kong, Tangiers, Paris and numerous other places but I had never ever seen a response such as I saw that night in Italy. Hundreds of New Testaments were distributed in a short space of time as well as other literature. The cry of the people was for the whole Bible, and did they not have the right to have the whole Bible? They had been denied access to God's Word for years in Russia, they knew nothing of their history and most did not understand what it meant to be a Jew.

At one meeting when the crowd was asked if they knew who Abraham was there was a silence and then one man spoke up and said, "He's my neighbour we came on the same train from the transit camp in Vienna." I must confess that it took some days for it to really dawn on me that here were Jews who did not know what it means to be a Jew. Most had never been to a synagogue or kept the traditional Sabbath observances, they had never been able to light the Friday night candles. Most of the men had never had a Bar Mitzvah service and under the oppressive regime of Soviet Russia it had been forbidden even to circumcise the baby boys. They were still Jews ethnically even if not religiously and the Russians had not allowed them to be assimilated. They have the features of the Jews and the characteristics of the Jews and, let us not, forget the Covenant that God gave to the Jews. His Covenant stands unchangeable although they know so little about it. There are a few exceptions; some people managed in Moscow and Leningrad to attend underground or clandestine gatherings and Yeshivot during the dark years. Apart from the big cities there was virtually no chance for them to learn anything about God. Jews who tried to attend services at the open churches were often told not to come back. Now at last they had the chance to receive the Bible and to learn of their heritage, should we not give them the whole Bible? I am convinced that it is their right.

Some friends advised me only to give them the New Testament for two reasons. Firstly, because if we gave them the whole Bible

they might begin to read at Genesis and never reach the New Testament. Secondly, because it is cheaper to produce New Testaments and
we could give three New Testaments for the price of one Bible. My
conviction is that since it is the work of the Spirit to reveal the Gospel
we can surely trust the Lord to lead the people to reach the New
Testament in His time. As to the cost factors, while we want to be
good stewards and use the Lord's money in the best possible way I
believe it would be false economy to deny these people the whole
Bible. After all the Jews are the people who gave it ALL to us in the
first place. So the challenge began to grow in my heart to do something
to supply the word of God to these people but how could I do it? Where
would I begin?

Each night when I returned to my room at the El-Paso I found it
difficult to sleep because of all the thoughts that were whirling round
and round in my head.

The next few days were a repetition of the first as we travelled up
and down the coast visiting seven different locations and seeing this
amazing phenomenon. In one area the people were living in a summer camp site in temporary wooden buildings. Now it might be a nice
place to camp in the summer with a crowd of young people but in
January it was a squalid place reminiscent of a concentration camp.
The perimeter is surrounded by wire fencing and there is a guard on
duty at the gate. His main function seems to be to keep people like us
from entering the camp to do our work. We did manage to enter and
walk around to see the conditions at first hand, the small shack like
buildings are shared by four families with one communal kitchen. The
sanitation is in blocks some distance away and is not exactly five star
luxury. Of course these people have not come from a land where they
ever had five star luxuries so the conditions are not so bad for them as
they would be for us.

After looking around the camp we went back to the car park
nearby where we had parked our vehicle under some trees.   In the lane
way leading to the car park we could see people living in cars and make
shift tents. Many of these people had come from Poland and Romania
and not being able to get a place in the camp had just parked
themselves outside. Joel was intending to have a meeting but the publicity material had been removed and the people did not know when
the meeting would be held. In this area there was a lot of resistance to

the work and soon we experienced some of it at first hand. While we had been walking through the camp some of our friends had been distributing literature from the van at the parking area and as we made our way back we met some people carrying our literature. I noticed a red haired boy rushing along in some excitement and looking very purposeful. We soon found out why. He was the son of a 'Rabbi' and had gone to tell his dad that the 'Missionaries' were giving out literature about Jesus.

In a short time we saw a man walking quickly through the camp coming in our direction, he was surrounded by some friends of his and before long they had arrived at our van. The 'Rabbi' began to object to our work and became rather agitated, it was then that he made his big mistake. Turning to the rapidly growing crowd he screamed, "The Christian's Bible says that Moses had horns." Several times he repeated this ridiculous statement and then some of the watching crowd began to turn against him. One lady said that he should have stayed in Russia where he belonged, that they were now free people who would talk to whom they pleased. The debate grew louder and I was longing to join in.

I realised however that even though the 'Rabbi' could speak English it would be pointless for us to debate as the people would not understand. Some one said that the 'Rabbi' was generating quite a lot of heat but not much light.

It was then that our friend Sam did something that was really quite wonderful for such a new believer, he went to the front of the van and returned with the Bible in his hand. Sam asked the 'Rabbi' if this was the 'Christian's Bible' and he replied that it was. "All right Rabbi," said Sam, "Show the people where it says Moses had horns." Of course the 'Rabbi' could not do any such thing and the people began to jeer at him so in a very short time he left the scene muttering to himself as he went. The altercation did not hinder our work indeed the 'Rabbi' helped to increase the crowd and the interest. The poor 'Rabbi' thought he was doing the work of the Lord by trying to hinder the 'Missionaries', we must not condemn him but rather pray for his salvation. He called himself 'Rabbi' but he had no formal training. He had already been to America for a few months where he had received some instruction in Judaism and was now at the camp trying to convert the atheistic Soviet Jews to make them into religious Jews. The people seemed to feel that they had been long enough under a system of rules and regulations and really they did not want to listen to him. That day I met an elderly lady and after a few moments of conversation she confided in me. In her carrier bag she had her pet cat that she had smuggled out of Russia. It had not been so difficult to get it to Italy but now she was worried in case it was not possible to take the cat to America or to Israel. The poor woman seemed to have no other friend in the world except that cat and she was really determined that if the cat was not able to travel further then she would just have to stay in Italy with it. I have often wondered what became of her.

When we returned to the centre I asked Joel some questions about the situation and what I could do to help with the work among the people. I was impressed with the urgency of the hour and the hunger for the Word of God. Joel told me that they needed Bibles in Russian and food and blankets and other material. I said that I would make no promises but that I would pray about it and we would see what the Lord would arrange. Joel expressed his delight at this response and told me that many Americans had come through and made big promises but then forgot all about them when they left Italy. Others wanted to take over the work and their offers of help were always with strings attached.

That night I returned to the El-Paso guest house where I was staying and asked the Lord what I should do about all this. In one more day I would be leaving Italy to return home to Northern Ireland and my normal work.

Would I just go home and return to the usual routine? Would I simply say that I had a wonderful few days among the Russian Jews in Italy but that now it was over? What would I do?

As I prayed the Lord directed me to the book of Nehemiah chapter thirteen where I read these words. "On that day they read in the book of Moses in the audience of the people; and therein was found written, that the Ammonite and the Moabite should not come into the congregation of God forever; BECAUSE THEY MET NOT THE CHILDREN OF ISRAEL WITH BREAD AND WITH WATER," Suddenly I realised that these ancient Ammonite and Moabite people had incurred the judgement of God because they did nothing to help the Children of Israel as they were on their journey from the Egyptian bondage to their Promised Land.

Now here they were on another exodus this time from the Soviet bondage and I could do something to help them on their way. I MUST come to meet them and bring them "bread and water" on the journey, I must do all I could to help these modern children of Israel in their time of need. A fire began to burn in my heart with a terrible intensity that was so fierce if I had not acted to do something I think it would have consumed me. Those who came near me in those next days felt it and one lady said, "That man is so much on fire with this thing that you will get burned if you go near him." I think that was really true for I could scarcely stand still and for the next ten days or so I was very difficult to live with and to work with, I wanted everything done NOW immediately with no delay.

Even as I boarded the plane in Rome to fly to London en route for Belfast I was considering what I could do to get things really moving. Where could I find Russian language Bibles? Where could I find the means to buy them? How could I get them to Italy? Who would help me? All these and many more questions flooded my mind.

At London's Heathrow airport I changed to the British Airways flight that would take me on to Belfast. Just after take off I was sitting absorbed in my thoughts when I saw a figure stand up and make a quick dash to the wash room, my reverie was interrupted as I said to myself, "I know that man".

I watched for the door to re-open and sure enough it was none other than Rev. Dr. Ian Paisley who emerged. I decided to go at once to speak to him and so made my way up to the front of the aircraft to his seat. Mr. Paisley looked up as I approached and I said, "Do you know me?" As he was not very sure I said, "Ronnie McCracken," to which he replied, "I know you, you are the Missionary to the Jews; where are you coming from brother?" When I said that I was coming from ROME he looked up quickly with more interest and boomed out, "WHERE?" I asked if he would mind my sitting beside him and I began to pour out the whole story of what I had seen. Mr. Paisley was deeply moved as he listened to my account and promised to encourage his people to pray. He even offered to raise the situation regarding the Russian Jews in the House of Commons at Westminster if I wanted him to. I was most encouraged by this meeting on the plane and by Mr. Paisley's reaction to what I had to say. He was the first one to hear something about what I had seen and experienced and if he reacted like this then others would too.

Our plane was soon landing at Aldergrove and my wife met me and drove me to our home. The first thing she heard from me was, "I don't care if I have to mortgage the house to do it but I am going back to Italy with Bibles for those people as soon as I possibly can." That very day I was to hold a get-together for a group of fifty people who were planning to go with me to Israel for our annual Easter-Passover tour.

I just arrived into my house, with the suitcase still in the entrance hall when the first people began to arrive. I felt a bit sorry for the people that day because every time I began to tell them the necessary details about our trip to Israel I found myself digressing to talk about the Soviet Jews in Italy. In spite of that they must have had enough information about Israel for they all turned up on the appointed day and we had a truly wonderful tour. Those people were the first to hear about the opportunity to get the Word of God to the Soviet Jews in Italy, apart from Dr. Paisley. Those people went out of our house that day and spread the news to their friends and to their churches and in a large measure they created the interest that was to be used by the Lord to meet the challenge of this unique opportunity.

It was my deep feeling that it was most urgent to act immediately, in a year or two these Russian Jews would become like all the rest and either be assimilated into secular society or else become religious. Either way once they reached their destination it would be more difficult to witness to them, besides they would be scattered all over America, Canada, and Australia and NEVER be together again. This was a unique time that required unique action. Even if I had to mortgage the house and even if it would take me all of the next twenty years to pay off the mortgage I was determined to do it in order to bless these people.

CHAPTER FIVE

Five Thousand Russian Bibles

First thing on Monday morning I got on the telephone to the Bible Society to see if I could locate some Russian Bibles. The first reaction was that it was not possible as the demand from Russia had been so large in recent days that the supply had been exhausted. It could be up to four or even six weeks before more would be available. I was anxious to get the Bibles to Italy within the next few days not within six weeks, so I was feeling a little frustrated. I then telephoned the other Bible Society only to be told that the man in charge of the Russian department was on holiday and would not be back for about ten days. If I could call back after that time then I could discuss the situation with him. I expressed the opinion that surely everything did not come to a halt just because someone was on holiday. I came away from the telephone feeling even more frustrated because I could not seem to get anything going and then I had a brain wave and said to myself, "What about the Faith Mission book shop in Belfast." That shop is famous for having just about everything in stock, and must be one of the best Christian book shops anywhere. I went back to the telephone and called the shop and asked to speak to Mr. Edward Douglas, the manager, as soon as Mr. Douglas came to the telephone I asked him if by any chance he had any Russian Bibles in stock. My heart sank as he said that although there had been a stock of Russian

Bibles they had all gone because people were buying them for posting to the Soviet Union. Mr. Douglas then asked me what it was all about and I explained a little to him over the phone. He then said, "Ronnie leave it with me for the next half hour and I will see what I can turn up." Now if Mr. Douglas cannot obtain a book for you then you may be sure that it cannot be found and similarly if it is available then he will be sure to find it. I left the matter with him in the knowledge that he would take prompt action for me.

However I could not just sit still and wait, I had another idea and I would have to pursue it. It meant travelling into Belfast and across the city to the East side. As I left home I felt more confident that we would be able to do something to meet the need. I drove across the city to the office of the Every Home Crusade where together with some other friends I was to discuss the possibility of producing a special edition of a Russian scripture booklet. W. E. Allen has done tremendous work over many years in producing Christian literature in many languages. He already had a set up for producing a Russian scripture booklet but I needed something a little different that would be more suitable for giving to Jews. We sat for a few moments in the office drinking a mug of tea and discussing things and then Mr. Allen asked me how many copies I wanted printed and when I replied, "FIFTY THOUSAND." Mr. Allen said, "Lets not waste time talking about it, lets get the press rolling and get them out." It took about three days before I received those fifty thousand booklets in a special format. On the front cover we had a Menorah and the flames on the candles spelled out the name of Jesus the Light of the world.

On the back cover we had the words of Isaiah chapter fifty-three in Russian. It is not merely words when I say that it really was miraculous that fifty thousand copies of such a Scripture portion booklet could be produced so quickly in East Belfast. It was while we were still in discussion at the office of the Every Home Crusade that the telephone rang and I received a message that I was to telephone the Faith Mission book shop as soon as possible. That telephone call was to present me with the biggest challenge to faith that I had ever experienced in my lifetime up to that moment. Mr. Douglas told me he had located FIVE THOUSAND RUSSIAN BIBLES but that I would need to tell him right away if I wanted them or not. For a moment I hesitated while faith trembled. I distinctly remember Rev. Robin Little who was in the office looking me in the eye from across the office desk at that moment, then the Lord seemed to say to me, "Remember the text I gave you from Ecclesiastes.............. 'It is good that thou shouldest lay hold of this, Yea also from this withdraw not thy hand.' Do not draw back. Do not withdraw your hand"

So I said to Mr. Douglas, "I will take the lot." His reply was encouraging and at the same time daunting, "They are on the way to you NOW, the cost is £3.95 each but we will let you have them for £2.00, so that will be £10,000 you owe to the Faith Mission." At that moment I really did not know from where or how we would find the thousands of pounds to pay for all the material we were ordering, but there was no way I could stop. The bill at the book shop rose to £11,282 before we completed all our purchases there. As we left the office of Every Home Crusade I was joined by Mr. Trevor Eves of Bangor, Trevor has been interested in evangelistic work overseas for many years. We decided to go to visit another printing works to discuss the possible production of a special newspaper format of the Gospel of Mark. We chose Mark simply because it was the shortest and because I had available a bilingual Russian/English text of Mark. Our idea was to produce it as a newspaper that would be reasonably cheap to print, and that would be easy to distribute and also light for the people to take with them when they would eventually move on. I specially wanted to be able to use it to give to those many people who were interested in learning English. The Soviet Jews in Italy mostly wanted to get to the U.S.A. where of course they would need to speak English. The majority of the people did not know the English language and there were few English text books available to them in Italy for study. My idea was to give them a bi-lingual paper that could assist them in learning English through being able to compare the Russian and English words side by side. At the same time as learning some English they would be getting the Gospel message that they really needed more than anything else. Mr. Eves and I made the journey to a little town in the County Down called Rathfriland to speak to the owner of the Outlook Press.

When we approached Vera McDowell she seemed a little doubtful at first if the work could be done in the short space of time available as the press was busy with regular work. After some deliberations and hesitations she advised me to go into the print shop where I could speak with the foreman printer about the work I wanted to have done and see what he decided.

Just as we entered the print shop through the front door a man in a grey nylon shop coat entered through a door at the rear. He glanced up and said, "Mr. McCracken, I am surprised to see you here." To my surprise I realised that this was a man I knew well and whom I had frequently seen when preaching at his church. I had never known what this man did for a living and presumed that he was a farmer. I was amazed to see him at the printing press. He told me that he had worked there for many years and asked me what I was doing there. I had never before been at the printing works, and indeed it was my first visit to Rathfriland. As I explained our idea about the Gospel newspaper and the doubts Vera had about whether or not it could be done in time he declared, "Mr. McCracken, I am the man who will be doing the work and if YOU need it then you will have it". We returned to the office to speak with Miss. McDowell about the work and after a few words I thought I had better be completely open about the situation to her. I stated, "I want the work done as soon as possible, but I must explain that this is a step of faith for which we have no money in hand to pay the bill." Without so much as batting an eyelid Vera McDowell replied, "Never mind, we will print it for you, and we'll say a prayer that the Lord will provide for your needs." What a tremendous encouragement that was to my heart that day. Within a few days I had the proofs and with only a few minor changes the text was printed and after three more days I had received TWENTY FIVE THOUSAND bilingual Gospel of Mark newspapers.

Again I feel it to be really miraculous that from a small printing works in a rural town in Northern Ireland they could turn out such a large quantity of Russian/English Gospel newspapers in so short a time. Mr Eves acted as delivery man and soon we had a huge pile of newsprint in the entrance hall of our home. If there had been time to plan everything properly we would have organised a store or hall to collect the materials but there was no opportunity for planning meetings in this unique time of challenge.

All the materials began to collect at our home and soon it became like a warehouse, for more than a week we had scarcely a chair to sit down on. As word began to spread around the country about our desire to get the Word of God to the Soviet Jews in Italy our telephone started to ring non-stop with calls from interested friends asking what they could do to help.

As a result we decided to call a short notice meeting on Saturday, January 27 1990 at Ballycraigy Congregational Church. Even before our meeting at Ballycraigy the friends at Rathcoole Baptist Church, where Pastor Tom Orr then led the fellowship asked me to come and inform them about the situation in Italy. I was most warmly received there by Pastor and people and the interest shown was again a tremendous encouragement to my heart. As the people left at the end of that meeting a young man passed me carrying a book in his hand. I could see that it was in Russian and immediately asked the young man if he could read Russian. When he replied that he could not I asked him why he had that Russian book with him. He explained to me that he had purchased the book to post it to someone in the Soviet Union some time. When I examined the book I could see that it was a beautifully illustrated children's Bible story book of the highest quality. I said to him, "You are going to give me that book for some little Jewish child from Russia." His reply was that he was going to post it to the Soviet Union and could not give it to me. I tried once more and said to him, "Do you know that it says in the Bible, 'To the Jew FIRST'." The young man immediately handed me the book without any further comment and later on the Lord multiplied that book into ONE THOUSAND illustrated Bible story books for children.

A few days later Mr. Douglas telephoned to say that the Russian Bibles had arrived and would I come at once and take delivery of them as there was no room in the shop to store them. I had to quickly organise some transport and Mr. Eves again stepped in to assist us by using his van. To speed things up I borrowed a cattle trailer from a local farmer to tow behind my own car. That trailer had carried many a valuable animal to and from the market but it never carried such a precious cargo before as it did that day. I do not suppose that the manufacturer or the owner for that matter ever imagined in their wildest dreams that it would be used to transport Russian Bibles for Jews in Italy!

As I was loading the trailer outside the shop in Belfast's Upper Queen Street, I was very grateful for the help of several of the workers. Nevertheless those parcels seemed to grow heavier and the journey from lorry to trailer longer each time. The Traffic warden was urging us to hurry as no parking is allowed in that area. So I was especially glad when a young man came along and offered to help us with the carrying, as he began to work I realised that it was another young man from Rathcoole Baptist Church. I must confess that when I saw the actual size of the pile of Bibles the realisation began to sink in that I had really bought all of these books and that I was entirely responsible to the Faith Mission for the bill. They were really mine. I would have to pay the Faith Mission for them. The thought of it made my faith waver and the devil tried to tell me that I would never be able to get out of debt for the rest of my life.

When we had loaded the last of the parcels into the trailer I went into the shop and Mr. Douglas leaned over the counter, he handed me a brown envelope and said, "As soon as possible please, Ronnie." Inside was the bill for TEN THOUSAND POUNDS made out to me. As I fully realised that I owed all that money to Mr. Douglas my faith began to waver even more. What if the Lord did not meet the need?, What if I could not get a mortgage on the house?, What if........? As I came out of the shop with the envelope in my hand the young man beckoned me into the trailer and said, "I want to help you with the purchase of these Bibles." He then proceeded to write a cheque for £150.00 that came like a promise from Lord to my heart saying to me that I did not need to worry for HE would not fail us. I had to return to the shop for a moment and as I entered Mr. Douglas said, "A certain man was in just now and he has paid £250.00 off your bill." So even at the moment when faith was wavering and doubt was growing even then the Lord strengthened and upheld me by His Omnipotent hand. Those two were really sent by the Lord at the right moment and I am deeply indebted to that young brother and to the other man for their obedience to the Lord. Not only did they obey the Lord but they did it at exactly the right time. They were some more of the 'ravens' that the Lord directed to sustain us in the time of need.

In a short time the Bibles were unloaded at my home and joined the Gospel of Mark newspapers in our entrance hall. Mr. Noel Reid the owner of 'Reid's the Florists', kindly collected the fifty thousand Scripture booklets for me from the Every Home Crusade and delivered them to our house. By now there was only a very narrow space to squeeze through in our hallway and people were arriving daily with more and more gifts of food. Our telephone was ringing to such an extent that we had to get British Telecom to install an extra line to our home so that we could make telephone calls without preventing incoming calls from reaching us.

It was necessary for us to make a lot of International calls to Italy, to France and to Germany as we tried to make all the arrangements regarding the purchase of other Russian literature. Then we had also to make all the necessary arrangements to be able to transport the goods through so many borders. Many hours were to be spent on the telephone to British customs at Dover to secure passage without having to pay enormous sums of tax duty. Information had to be faxed from Italy to me to secure clearance through the Italian border without payment of import duties. So many channels had to be gone through, it was just as well that I had no experience of doing this kind of thing, I had no idea of all the rules and regulations and European community requirements. I just walked blindly on in faith not knowing how really impossible it was to succeed to deliver all of this material to Italy.

THE BALLYCRAIGY MEETING

We had decided to ask our own home church at Ballycraigy if we could have the use of the premises for a short notice or emergency meeting on Saturday night January 27 1990 and we are very grateful to our minister and the deacons for their co-operation. We mailed out a number of invitations to those we knew were interested in our work and telephoned as many friends as we could in the short space of time available. Our idea was to gather some interested people and to share with them my experiences in Italy and see what the Lord would do. On the Wednesday before the meeting we had the heaviest snowfall of the entire winter and we felt a bit anxious about the conditions. If the snow persisted then many would not be able to get to the meeting.

Even though we did feel a certain anxiety, at the same time there was a deep peace and a certainty that all would be well for the Lord was in this thing and He would not fail us. Before Saturday night the thaw set in and the snow vanished leaving a wet bedraggled country-side behind it but without any serious hazard for travellers. We arrived very early at the Church that Saturday night but only to find that many were already there before us and soon cars began to arrive from all directions. To our pleasant surprise the church at Ballycraigy was crowded and several had to be accommodated on extra seating in the aisle. The meeting got off to a great start with wonderful singing that set the scene for a time of special blessing. We taught the congregation a little chorus whose words I had written a few years earlier:

> "Dear Lord don't forget them, they're Thy Chosen people,
> Long scattered in exile and now far from Thee.
> In Thy loving kindness, at last bring them to HIM.
> Dear Lord, please remember, dear Lord; Save the JEW."

Mr. Sammy Campbell the organist of Abbots Cross Congrega-tional Church, had helped by setting these simple words to the music of 'Annie's Song'. I must be one of the most unmusical people in the world and my tuneless singing is well known so I could not find music suitable for singing the words. Sammy on the other hand seems to be just full of music. How wonderfully the congregation sang the simple chorus to the tune of 'Annie's Song' that night. It was like a special prayer to the Lord for the Russian Jews that evening. The minister of Ballycraigy Church, Pastor Tom Shaw, suggested that we should take up an offering during the service. Normally it is my practice only to leave a basket at the door for a retiring offering as the people leave our meetings.

That night the building was very crowded and some people would leave by different doors. At the end of this unique service there would be many friends to talk to and greet. We had not really given any thought to what we should do about a collection but when Mr. Shaw suggested that we should pass around a collection plate it seemed like a good idea. That way we would avoid any confusion at the end of the meeting.

During the meeting at Ballycraigy the Lord touched many hearts and we were truly amazed to find at the end that in that one offering more than thirteen thousand pounds was donated. In more than thirty years of Christian service I had never experienced any thing like this before, we did not ask or beg or plead for money, we made no appeal to the people for funds, this was the freewill giving of people whose hearts the Lord had touched. Truly it was the Lord's doing and it is marvellous in our eyes. How we praise the Lord for the wonderful miracle of His provision. Yes, it is true; God's 'ravens' still fly. Sometimes they may literally be ravens while at other times they take human form. Sometimes they may be sent to the brook Cherith and sometimes it might be to Ballycraigy church. Sometimes they have wings and sometimes they are elderly ladies in coats and hats but they are still God's 'ravens', and He uses them to meet the need. I am grateful to all the 'ravens' who came to Ballycraigy that Saturday night, they fed us in the time of need just like their counterparts did for the Tishbite long ago. They sustained us and refreshed us and they renewed our strength just when our resources were exhausted. Just when it seemed that the brook was dry they poured out their love to preserve us. I wish I could say 'Thank you' to them all.

What a wonderful night for us to remember, a night when God's 'ravens' brought the means to supply the Bread of Life to the thousands of Russian Jews then passing through Italy. How our hearts were singing the praise of God that night as well as our mouths. During the meeting I showed the people the Illustrated Children's Bible I had captured at Rathcoole Baptist. I expressed a desire to have at least one thousand of them and said if I could find one thousand copies I would buy them. The following Thursday morning a telephone call from the continent gave me the name and telephone number of a man who could possibly supply me at short notice with a similar book. I telephoned at once to Mr. Bill Kapitaniuk at the Slavic Gospel Association printing press in France and after only a few moments of conversation he agreed to let me have one thousand copies of an illustrated "Life of Christ."

Then we discussed how I would get them to Italy. I said I would send our transport via the printing works at Marpent and they would pick up the books.

A question was raised about unsealing the truck and we thought that we might have to have a French customs officer come to break the seal and then to remake it. It sounded like a lot of extra red tape but I

was determined to get those books for the children no matter how difficult it might be. Almost as an afterthought I asked Philip Kapitaniuk,
Bill's son, how much the books would cost me and he replied that they
would be fifteen French Francs each. This was extra expenditure just
when we were beginning to see a way to clear all the accounts. My
wife, who is much more practical about these things than I am, was a
little anxious when she arrived home from her work at the hospital and
found I had ordered yet more books.

That very same evening just as we tried to clear a place in our
dining room to have our evening meal with the family, there came a
knock at our front door. Now it was absolutely impossible to get anyone in by our front door for the place was blocked with Russian Bibles,
Gospel Newspapers, Scripture Booklets, Blankets and other material. I
had to shout to the person to come to the back door and soon a man
wearing a pair of overalls came to the kitchen door. He was on his way
to do a repair job for the weather was very stormy and power lines
were down cutting off electricity to many farms in our district. This
brother was on his way to do some emergency work but stopped to see
me for a few moments. He began by telling me that he had been trying
to get to see me for a few days but had been hindered and then asked
me what was happening. I told him a little of the story as we sat
perched on the edge of a sofa piled high with blankets waiting to be
sorted, all around us were bags of clothes.

Although we had pleaded with people NOT to bring us used clothing the generous hearted Ulster folk still brought it along. I kept saying, "I cannot give a nuclear physicist from Russia someone's second
hand pair of trousers." Actually we simply did not have the time to sort
through piles of used clothing and itemise it. Most of what we did
receive we managed to deal with but a lot of midnight oil was burned
before we were finished. As we sat talking together the man said, "I
want to know what has been happening TODAY." I told him about
ordering the thousand books for the children and as I did he immediately said, "That is why I am here. I have been trying to get here for
a few days but could not make it until today. I am to buy those thousand books." From his pocket he took out three separate cheques each
one already written and for a different amount. One on behalf of his
wife, one if I remember rightly on behalf of his son, and the other for

himself. We had no idea at that moment about the rate of exchange for the Sterling pound against the French Franc. My visitor could not have known anything about my purchasing the books or their cost.

When I contacted the bank next day to check the exchange rate I found he had given me exactly the right amount needed to pay the bill for those thousand books. I suppose that I should not have been surprised for the Lord knew all about the rates of exchange and the cost of the books. Oh yes! God's 'ravens' still fly. That brother was one of God's 'ravens' who came that night to supply us with the means of putting ONE THOUSAND illustrated LIFE OF CHRIST books into the hands of Russian Jewish children. All I did was to pass along the gift and I had the privilege of sharing in the wonderful thing God was doing. Later I will write of how the Lord gave us nine thousand more of those wonderful books for the children. It was a particular joy for me to see the children receive the message of the Lord Jesus Christ. Jesus took the children in His arm long ago even when others would have sent them away. It was a special privilege to be able to bless the Russian Jewish children.

CHAPTER SIX

The Miracle Of The Meal

When Elijah was waiting there at Cherith during the drought the brook eventually ran dry. Without water even the miraculous provision of food brought by the Ravens could not sustain him. The Lord had made other arrangements for His servant Elijah. He was told to go to Zarephath to the home of a widow woman. The Lord was very specific about where he was to go and told him, "I have commanded a widow woman there to feed you." When the prophet arrived at Zarephath he found a tragic situation, as he asked for water and then for a piece of bread the widow woman poured out her heart. She explained that she was down to her last handful of meal and that she had decided to use it to make a little cake of bread for herself and her son. They would eat their very last meal together and then prepare to die for all they had was gone. The extremes of the drought and the resulting famine had dried up her hope and death seemed inevitable.

It must have seemed to her like a ridiculous request when Elijah asked her to first of all bake a little cake for him. I suppose most people would have refused in such circumstances, most would have said that they had not enough for themselves. This woman remembered the command of the Lord and fulfilled the request of the prophet. That was when the miracle of the meal happened, the little handful in the bottom of the barrel never failed, miraculously it was replenished every day. Each time she drew it out to bake the last cake the Lord wonderfully replaced it with just enough for one cake more. Here is one of the principles of faith unveiled in the Old Testament. The Lord did not fill the barrel up for her, as He could so easily have done.

It would have been no harder for the Lord to give her all the meal she needed for the rest of the famine in one go. The Lord supplied just the amount she needed each day no more no less. I have often wondered what would have happened if she had refused the man of God. If she and her son had selfishly baked and eaten their little cake themselves it would surely have been the last meal they would ever have eaten. That poor woman was in great need but she gave all she had, not just to Elijah, but to Elijah's God. As a result Elijah's God took care of her until after the famine was over, yes and after it too. I have an idea that if she had been given a full barrel of meal she would have been in difficulties. The starving neighbours would likely have stormed the house to get it, but everyone knew that the widow had only a handful left so there was no point in going to attack her. Throughout all the rest of the famine the Lord just replaced the handful over and over again in His own wonderful way.

The Lord is able to meet every need we have right away, but sometimes He lets us wait a while for the provision. God's provision is always perfect.

It is always just enough to meet the present need, for if we had too much we might become self sufficient and find ourselves in difficulties. We can learn so much from the miracle of the meal barrel that never failed and the little cruse of oil that kept on pouring out. Each day as the poor widow poured out the meal and the oil the dear Lord poured more in. We also experienced a miracle of the meal; only for us it was porridge meal that came from the heart of County Armagh.

When I had asked Pastor Joel what kind of things would be useful for him to give to the people one of the items he mentioned was what the Americans call Quick Oats. So when I was asked in turn by many people in Northern Ireland what would be useful to send to the Russian Jews I told them porridge. Many people were calling at our home bringing various gifts as they were exercised by the Lord. It became necessary to work late into the night trying to organise all the materials and to sort through them. Someone very kindly sent a carton of packet soups but they proved to be a variety called pea and ham. Even though the Russian Jews were in the main non kosher, it still would not do for me to send them pea and ham soup! We had to be very careful not to cause offence unwittingly. The pea and ham carton was exchanged at the Cash and Carry for a more suitable flavour. This kind of thing meant that everything had to be sorted and examined individually before being packed.

One Tuesday evening I was busy packing cartons and sorting through materials right to the last possible moment before I had to leave home. Every month we have a meeting for fellowship and prayer in the Woodvale-Ardoyne area of Belfast, this area has suffered much during the troubles but we like to maintain our meeting there. It was due to be held on that Tuesday evening and it must have been about ten minutes before the meeting when I dashed out to the car to rush to the meeting place. I had been working in our drawing room packing bags of porridge into cartons until just before I left home. As I went racing off along the road in a big hurry to get to the meeting on time the Lord suddenly spoke to me. Now I did not hear an audible voice but it was an inner voice that said, "Why are you fiddling around with those small bags of porridge? telephone the factory in the morning." I must confess that I was really startled by this and as I drove along the road I said, "Lord was that really you or is this my imagination?"

The Lord said to me again, "Telephone the factory in the morning." I had no idea as to where in the world the porridge factory might be located. Although porridge is a nutritious and healthy food and is said to be an excellent thing to eat for all kinds of reasons, I am not very fond of it myself.

I think that may be due to the fact that in my student days we had a daily diet of porridge for breakfast. Unfortunately our cook had no idea of how to make porridge and it was always somewhat burned and lumpy. I struggled so much to swallow my portion every morning in those student days in Manchester. I made a kind of vow that when I would leave college there would be no more porridge for me. I have largely kept to that promise. Really I had no idea where the factory could be where porridge was manufactured and I had never in my life ever given it so much as a thought. That night when I eventually arrived home from the meeting the first thing I did was to go and look at one of the packets of porridge. I found the name of the factory and then looked in the telephone directory for the phone number. Later when I went upstairs to go to bed I told my wife what had happened and that I must phone the factory next morning. Pat gave a kind of sleepy sigh and said, "What will you be at next." I replied that I did not know but I was certain of one thing, I had to call that factory or I would be disobedient to the Lord. Next morning I telephoned to the factory and asked to speak to someone, I did not really know what to say or exactly why I was telephoning except that the Lord had told me to do it. At first I spoke to a girl at the office who then transferred me to a gentleman so that I could explain what I wanted to him. As he came to the phone I said, "This is Ronnie McCracken speaking," and he immediately interrupted and said, "I know you, I heard you preaching one time in Portadown. I was one of the victims who had to sit and listen to you."

This little bit of good natured banter, which is a very typical Northern Ireland introduction, really put me at ease. I felt more confident to speak when the man asked what I was calling for and what he could do for me. Still it was a little hesitantly that I explained that I hardly knew exactly why I was calling. I began to outline what we were trying to do to help the Jewish refugees from Russia and concluded by saying, "I was wondering if there would be any chance of my buying a ton of porridge meal direct from the factory. If I could buy it from you it would save me having to go to the supermarket or the Cash and Carry." After I had spoken with the man on the other end of the line he replied and said, "No I am sorry, but there is no way you can buy anything directly from our factory." I began to feel a bit disappointed and somewhat confused within myself but then he went on to say something else. "There is no way you can buy it BUT I will give it to you free of charge." I could not keep back the tears from my eyes when he said it, how wonderful is the Lord. Here was another of God's 'ravens' bringing not just a little bread but a TON of porridge meal. The next Thursday morning a lorry arrived at my home carrying forty-five huge bags of porridge meal. Our son Michael had a day off school and I was glad to enlist his help as a porridge carrier.

When Pat arrived home from her work at the hospital that day the large sacks of porridge had joined all the other things in our hallway and were stacked up to the ceiling, how we rejoiced together at what the Lord had done. The God who supplied His servant Elijah at the brook through the instrumentality of the ravens is still the same. The God who supplied His servant with the meal through the widow of Zarephath is still the same.

He supplied a ton of porridge meal for the Russian Jewish refugees in a way we could not have imagined. The Lord supplied in a way we could not have engineered even if we had tried. This time His agent was the owner of Speedicook Oats Ltd from the little town of Tandragee. I had often been in Tandragee to speak at various meetings but I really never knew that it was there they manufactured porridge meal. I will certainly never forget it in the future. Later I was to understand just how great a miracle the Lord was bringing to pass but at this stage a great deal was hidden from my eyes. I had no idea of all the rules and regulations that govern the movement of foodstuff in the European Community, I did not know that it is almost impossible to transport food aid of this kind successfully through so many borders. In His mercy the Lord concealed the difficulties from me and only revealed many of the obstacles after the materials had been delivered. Oatmeal is subject to special regulations but the Lord wonderfully by-passed them all and enabled us to deliver this good and nutritious food.

It was while our house was filled with all the good things that the Lord had sent that something truly wonderful happened. My father, who lived in the house next door, often dropped in to see what was going on. As he viewed the house in surprise he would say to me, "What are you doing to the house, how can Patricia put up with this." When my dad was looking around the house he saw the huge pile of Bibles and Gospels and he asked me, "Ronnie how are you going to pay for all this son." I told him that I really did not know but that I was sure that the Lord who owned the cattle on a thousand hills would not fail us. My poor old dad would shake his head and say that it seemed very strange to him. My dad was not a Christian and he found difficulty in understanding what was going on. All his life he had never shown much interest in spiritual things and I suppose it was very hard for him to realise that the Lord was leading us every step of the way. Then one morning he came to the kitchen door and spoke to me, in his hand he held some bank notes that he proceeded to give me. It was some of his old age pension that he had saved. "Here take this to help you pay for some of those Bibles," he said. How my heart rejoiced at this expression of love. It was the first time he had ever done such a thing. Surely the Lord was working in his heart after all the long years of praying.

I went to prayer with renewed enthusiasm and faith, that after thirty-two years of asking Him the Lord was really going to answer my prayers. Shortly afterwards the Faith Mission pilgrims came to hold a mission in our area at Ballyhill.

One day Mr. Willie Porter was passing along our road inviting people to the mission and saw my dad out working in his garden. Willie stopped to ask him to come to the mission but my dad asked him to come into the house as he wanted to speak to him. About ten minutes later Mr. Porter came running round to my house and said to me, "Ronnie rejoice, for I have just pointed your father to the Lord. Run round quick and speak to him." I had waited for thirty-two years to hear this good news so I decided not to run right away. Next morning I went to the greenhouse to pick a few tomatoes and took them to my father. As I knocked on the door he opened and said to me, "You had better come in for I have something I want to tell you." I entered the house and sat down and he told me the news I had longed and waited to hear for so many years. "I have done it at last, I have trusted the Lord to Save me" was what he said. How we rejoiced together at the goodness of the Lord. It was seeing the Lord's answers to prayer and His wonderful provision for all the Bibles and His supply of all the food that had finally melted my father's heart.

Something else came to hand that brought us tremendous joy when we received it. At one of our meetings I had mentioned in passing that we had been distributing sweets and candy to the children at the various centres in Italy. Brother Joel would say to us, "Only one candy per child. "So the lovely little Jewish children would receive one sweet. Those children were so beautiful, very often clinging to their mothers skirts just too shy to come to us. Sometimes I would play with a few of them some simple game for which we did not need words. How we longed to be able to tell them of the love of Jesus, I kept saying,

"If Pat was here she would have a Good News Club started in a few moments. Maybe she could use the wordless book." A friend who was at the meeting picked up what I said about the sweets and passed the word to another person who as far as know I had never met. One evening a car turned into our backyard but there seemed to be something strange about the vehicle as it approached the house. It was another 'raven' winging its way to us. The headlights were illuminating the top of the trees instead of the roadway for the car was weighted down at the rear, that car was loaded with sweets of all kinds for the children. The man whom I had never met, donated enough sweets from his business to fill seven tea chests to the brim. The confectionery was loose in cartons so we had to organise a team of volunteers to come and package the sweets. A group of ladies came to work for several days at our home, packing sweets into small plastic bags. Each little bag was prepared with love in Jesus name.

Each little bag contained a selection of different kinds of sweets, just enough for one child. The ladies enjoyed many happy hours as they worked in this pleasant task. What blessed fellowship and harmony in the Lord bound them together in this lovely work. So many lives were touched through this project, not only those who received the sweets, but also those who worked so hard to send them. We could not have done without those 'ravens' who supplied and those who worked to prepare everything for the long journey to Italy.

That was now quickly becoming my most serious concern. How were we going to get everything transported to Italy? Some friends who were trying to be helpful spoke about one way and some of another, the names of several large haulage companies were mentioned to me with a suggestion that I should approach them. One man kindly offered to supply a container for us to fill which he would then ship to Italy for us.

The Lord kept telling me that this would not be the way by which we would transport the goods He had sent to us. It was not going to be taken to a haulage company and just sent away. How was I going to get it delivered? I wanted to get everything on the way to Italy as soon as possible. The Jews were arriving almost daily but others too were leaving almost daily on their way to different destinations. Once the people moved on from Italy we would no longer be able to reach them. The big question was how could I actually get all these good things transported to Italy? The Lord had told me how I was not to send it. What I really urgently needed to know now was in which way I was to do it.

CHAPTER SEVEN

"On The Road, Frank"

With all the materials assembled at our home the most press-ing need was this question of how to go about making the arrangements to get everything on the road to Italy as soon as possible. Our priority was to get the Word of God to the Russian Jewish people before they would move on to other places. Once they were scattered all across America, Canada, and Israel we would never have a chance like this to reach them. Never again would these people be together all in one place in such circumstances; this was a unique time of opportunity. While I certainly felt that it was necessary to assist them in every way that we could with their practical needs, our aim was very clear. We wanted to give to them the Word of God so that they might find the Messiah, our Saviour. I often said, "There is not much point in giving a man a Bible if he needs a blanket to cover himself." By the same token there is not much point in our giving a man only a blanket for a covering when he really needs a covering for his sins.

I wanted to give them Bibles and blankets, Scriptures and sweets; all of them given as an expression of love in the Name of Jesus the Messiah. The people were in need of help but they were not perishing from hunger. The thing which concerned me most was that they were perishing spiritually. All of the money we received as gifts was expended in purchasing Christian literature for the people and getting it to them. We did not buy even one single item to assist in meeting the practical needs of the Russian Jews. Everything we took as material aid was freely donated by interested friends. The small packets of porridge, given from such generous hearts, as well as the ton of meal from the factory, were all gifts and we did not have to purchase any foodstuffs for the people. All the finance given was used to get the Word of God into the hands of the people. What a wonderful privilege to give thousands of copies of God's Word to people who had NEVER in their lives seen or handled a Bible.

The biggest question occupying my mind was exactly how to go about getting the transport organised. Much prayer went into this aspect of the project as I sought the Lord for guidance as to His will. One evening as I prayed the Lord brought to mind an old friend of boyhood days. Frank Bell and I had been in many an escapade in the old days before either of us knew the Lord. After I was converted I encouraged Frank to come to our meetings and for a short time we were students together at Bible college. Then for a long number of years we seemed to loose touch and seldom ever saw each other. The old acquaintance had been renewed when Frank invited us to be present at his daughter's wedding. We had been so pleased to go and it was wonderful to meet all the old friends again. Quite some time had passed again since the wedding without us having seen each other as we were both very busy with our work.

I had learned at the wedding that Frank was in the removal business, had several lorries and a number of men working for him. The Lord now vividly brought Frank before me and I knew that he would be the one to transport the materials to Italy.

It took a bit of searching to come up with his telephone number but eventually I found it. When I called him on the telephone we exchanged the usual pleasantries and then I asked him if he was very busy with his work. Frank told me that he was very busy and I then asked him if all his lorries were busy. By this time he began to realise that this was not just a social call to discuss how busy we each were. "Do you want to move house." Frank asked me. I replied. "No, I have no intention of moving house but I do need some things moved as soon as possible." Frank immediately offered to move anything for me that I needed moved.

I don't think he was really expecting my next comment though and when I said I needed something removed to Italy there was a pause. Then after a few moments Frank spoke and said, "That will be all right the Lord has told me that I have to do this and if I need to hire in a vehicle for the job I will do it." How my heart rejoiced to know for certain that all the things given with such love, and the Scriptures provided so miraculously, would arrive safely at the intended destination. I had heard stories of aid being donated and sent off but never reaching the people it was intended for. I was determined that this would not happen to our food and Bibles and that was why I needed a good friend to transport it.

Frank Bell was the answer to my prayers and without a doubt was another 'raven' commanded by God to bring the Bibles and donated materials to Italy. How I thank the Lord for the privilege of labouring together in this work. The next question was, how soon could we get the lorry on the road. Frank at first had the idea that he could do the job in about two weeks. TWO WEEKS! I wanted that material to be in Italy within a few days. ONE WEEK would be too long! I did not want any delay and everything was being prepared to depart at the first possible moment. We needed to pack and itemise every single thing. There had to be a detailed manifest of the goods going on the truck for the authorities. Actually this proved to be one of the most difficult things to do for every time I had the list typed someone else turned up with more items. I just couldn't say take it away I have typed the list. Even after the final typing of the manifest some friends arrived with more materials. Eventually we did have to say, "That's it, no more can go on this truck." I wanted everything on the road to Italy as soon as possible if not sooner.

To help him with the long journey Frank enlisted a friend to be his co-driver, this friend proved to be a real asset to the whole venture. He had wide experience of driving on the Continent and knew all the angles. He and I spent one whole day in my study with both phone lines busy as we spoke to various Government departments and customs officials about the red tape. We had some anxious moments when the insurance company baulked at the thought of covering the lorry for the journey but even in those moments the assurance that all was in the Lord's hands was our stay. Once all the arrangements were made we decided to load up the lorry on Saturday February 3.

It was arranged that we would hold a service of dedication and prayer after which the drivers would set off for the boat to Stranraer. That Saturday morning Frank brought the lorry and parked it in our back yard and before long the workers arrived to help us load all the materials on board. It was a wonderful day for us as we saw the dream becoming a reality. Here were all these 'ravens' rushing backwards and forwards through all the rooms of our house carrying those love gifts to the lorry. Oh yes, our carpets got a bit of extra wear and some of the doors got scratched as the tea chests were hauled out. It was still glorious to be doing this work for the Lord and for His ancient people, the Jews. Some of those helpers fetched and carried and some made tea to help keep the workers working, and soon all the things that had filled our house were gone. Afterwards it was clean up time and some of the ladies helped Pat to hoover and dust and get the house ship shape again.

We had only just managed to get everything tidied when people began to arrive for the dedication service. We wanted to pray for a safe journey and for the passage through the borders and customs. Most of all we wanted to pray that those Bibles and books would all be used by the Lord in a mighty way. The little service was simple and yet beautiful, it was a time of thanksgiving for answered prayer and a time of looking to the Lord for blessing on the way ahead. During the service I read a letter to the people that I had attached to the manifest of the cargo. I reproduce it here.

To Whom it may concern

"All the goods in this lorry are in free circulation in the European Community and are FREELY DONATED for charitable purposes to assist the Russian Jewish Refugees at present in TRANSIT through ITALY. It would be appreciated if all concerned could assist the speedy passage of these materials to their destination. Our Christian friends in Northern Ireland have donated these goods to help those who are suffering upheaval at this time. We in Northern Ireland have an all too profound knowledge of what it means to suffer.

These goods are donated in the Name of God to bring comfort to these Russian Jewish people as they are in transit. They are of no commercial value in that they are not to be sold for gain. All the materials are to be FREELY DISTRIBUTED. Mr. Bell and his helper are volunteers who are transporting the materials for us without hire or reward. Your co-operation with us and with the Lord in this project will be gratefully appreciated. God Bless you."

This was the letter we attached to the list of material we were sending on the lorry.

4 Tea Chests of Tea plus 4 cartons of Tea
1 Tea Chest of Coffee Plus 3 cartons of Coffee
3 Tea Chests of packet soups, desserts etc. plus 1 carton
1 Carton of Milk Powder
1 Carton of powdered soups
1 Carton of biscuits
1 Tonne Quick Oats (Porridge)
+ Cartons Quick oats
7 Tea chests mixed confectionery
4 Tea chests donated clothing
24 Cartons clothing/donated
40 Bales of Blankets
5,000 BIBLES in RUSSIAN LANGUAGE
25,000 Gospel of Mark Newspapers in RUSSIAN/ENGLISH
50,000 Scripture Booklets in Russian.

These were the materials we loaded on to the truck and which Frank was going to deliver to Italy. We really did need to pray that Saturday, for it is not easy to import anything into Italy. Just as our little service came to an end the telephone rang and someone asked to speak to the driver. When he came from the telephone he said that someone had called to tell him not to buy tickets for the ferry as they were already paid for. An anonymous friend had covered the cost for the return crossing from Larne to Stranraer and from Dover to Calais for the lorry. I still do not know the name of that anonymous 'raven' who decided to help us but I am so thankful. That was a tremendous help and a very real encouragement as the men prepared to set off for the long drive to Italy.

As we came out of the house after the service into the bitterly cold February day to bid the drivers God speed I picked up a bottle of sweets that had been left in our living room. We had tried to get it into a tea chest but it did not fit and so it had been left aside. As the lorry began to drive out of our back yard I tossed that bottle of Oatfield Chocolate Eclairs into the cab and shouted to the drivers.

"Take that with you for if it is left here my children might eat them and I don't want that. You can suck as you drive and it will help you to keep between the hedges."

How quiet and empty the house seemed when everyone had gone, how empty everywhere looked. It was not empty for long though for after a couple of hours the young people began to arrive for a youth meeting and soon the house was filled again, this time with lively young people.

I fully expected that the lorry would not reach the Continent before Monday at the earliest. It would likely be Monday morning before they could clear the English customs formalities at Dover and secure a needed T2 form for the European Community requirements. I was to fly out to Italy on Monday morning to commence negotiations with the Italians to try and secure the import permission in advance of the arrival of the lorry.

It was therefore a big surprise to receive a telephone call from a breathless Frank at lunch time on Sunday. Frank asked me to phone his wife and tell her that he had no time to telephone as he had to get on the next boat to France. The men had taken my words to heart when I said I wanted that material to get to Italy without any delay. They had driven all through the night without stopping, taking turns at the wheel and had arrived at Dover a day early. It would still have been impossible for them to cross to France until Monday morning except for one fact that was to speed them on their way. On entering the customs area to attempt getting the necessary clearance the official on duty was someone whom the drivers knew. That acquaintance coupled with my letter accelerated what we thought would be a lengthy process. Instead of having to wait for clearance on Monday morning it was granted right away and the men were told to drive straight on to the boat at once. Frank had dashed to the telephone to try and call me just as the ferry was ready to sail. Again it was a time for rejoicing at our home, we had wished the men God speed as they set off and how the Lord was speeding them. Later we came to understand that this was all in God's perfect timing as He arranged details which at that moment we were totally unaware of.

Praise the Lord that He had a 'raven' there in Dover on duty that day to speed the truck on its way to the Continent. Getting straight on to the boat with the needed forms meant that by six o'clock the lorry was in Calais a full day ahead of our planned schedule. When the lorry drove ashore in France there was a customs inspection and passport formalities. Frank was informed that there would be a delay of several hours. Heavy trucks were being held back until after 10 o'clock in order not to congest the roads around the port.

After they had been in the compound for a few minutes a French customs officer came to inspect the papers. As he stood up on the step of the lorry he could look into the cab and there he saw our jar of Oatfield sweets. "Ah English sweets, I love English sweets," he said. With typical Ulster hospitality Frank asked if he would like some and proceeded to tip about half the jar into his hat. The little French man was so delighted to get them that he was profuse in his thanks and said, "No need to wait longer, you can proceed at once on your journey." Those four extra hours were also to prove vital later on. It was certainly not "bribery and corruption" with chocolate eclairs, but the Lord really did use those sweets to speed the truck on its way to the next stop. The sweets actually came from Letterkenny in County Donegal but that was not something Frank felt he should point out to the French official with a taste for English sweets!

Leaving the compound the drivers followed the directions they had been given to get to a little town on the Belgian border called Marpent. The Slavic Gospel Association had a printing works there where a Ukrainian brother produced the illustrated Life of Christ books for children. Bill Kapitaniuk and his son Philip work 'flat out' to produce not only Russian but Polish and Romanian and other versions of this useful book. I particularly wanted one thousand of those books for distribution to the children and had instructed the drivers that they were to go at all costs to Marpent to collect them.

We had anticipated that the lorry would be sealed by British customs at Dover and that we would need French customs to come to

Marpent to break the seal. After loading up the extra thousand illustrated children's books at the printing press the French customs would probably reseal the lorry for transit through France.

Thankfully the lorry had not been sealed at all and that meant there was no need to try and find a French customs official at Marpent. Another possible delay was avoided and this was to prove of vital importance later in Italy. At the Slavic Gospel Association printing works the men were very warmly received and given a chance to rest a little before travelling on. Bill and Philip Kapitaniuk had never ever met me, and yet they trusted us to take those one thousand books without money being paid. I had offered to send it with the lorry if necessary but they told me not to worry about it at present, they would send the account to me in due course. In the end I purchased additional books from them and our final bill was about one hundred thousand French Francs. We are so grateful to the Slavic Gospel Association for all their help and trust.

When some other organisations refused to make literature available to us at any price because reaching Jews was not the priority of their mission, the Slavic Gospel Association provided me with what I needed and gave me every possible encouragement.

Once the additional books were loaded the drivers began the long haul through France and up to the Mont Blanc tunnel for the crossing into Italy. This was February and if there had been much snow they could have had to make a long and time consuming detour through the South of France. That winter the weather was mild in France and there was little snow on the road. In some places there was not even enough snow for the skiers on the mountains. So it did not prove to be too difficult to get up to the platform on Mont Blanc and drive through the long tunnel to reach the Italian border. This high mountain road can be very difficult if the weather turns nasty and certainly cars and trucks would need snow chains to get through.

All along the way the men had wonderful opportunities to witness to the long distance lorry drivers they met. When other drivers would ask them what load they were carrying they were often surprised to hear that our men were hauling Russian Bibles to Italy. Only eternity will reveal the outcome of those conversations.

The men made their way through France and over the Alps to Italy while I remained at home in Ireland for two more days during which time I visited some churches and urged our people to pray for the whole project. On Monday morning I flew to London and then on to Italy to try and smooth their way. Frank had given me a name and address when he telephoned from Dover but somehow it was a bit distorted. Just as Mr. Wong's address had been wrong through translation difficulties so now the address I was given where we should clear customs was not correct. That was something I didn't learn though, until the next day.

CHAPTER EIGHT
"Back To Italy"

My flight from London was delayed and I did not reach Fiumicinio airport until later than expected. Then I had to wait a long time to complete the formalities for a rented car. It was already dark before I set out for Ladispoli to meet Joel and the team. There was to be a meeting for the Russian Jews that night in a rented theatre and I was expecting to arrive in time to attend that meeting. As it was the meeting was over long before I arrived and the team had just concluded a prayer meeting as I rolled up. "Hi Ronnie, we thought you weren't coming at all," Joel greeted me, as I stepped from the car. I beckoned to Joel to come over to the car as I wanted to give him something right away. I realised that they would need to rent some storage space for the materials we were bringing and that vehicles would be needed to transport it to different centres. Cars and vans do not run on air so there would be fuel to buy and many additional expenses to meet. So as well as bringing the material I had also brought a substantial sum of money in the form of a bank draft. This would help with the work and also enable Joel to assist some of the needy families with rent for apartments and so on. I was anxious to get the draft delivered as soon as possible so I wanted to give it to Joel right away. As I passed the draft to him he glanced at it and then I could see tears in his eyes, after a moment he said to me, "Do you know what we have just been doing? We have had a prayer meeting about our finances. Our budget for the entire year of 1990 is already used in the first two months and we have been praying for the Lord's provision. Without this gift we would have had to cut back on the work and the insurance on the mini-bus is also due to be paid. This is surely a gift from the Lord." As Joel spoke I suddenly realised that the Lord had given to me the wonderful privilege to be one of His 'ravens' and to carry sustenance to His servants. How very wonderful is the Lord, His ways are past finding out.,

A place was found for me to lodge for the next few days with Danny and Ellen. They were a young couple from the United States who had been sent for a field term in Italy. The Jewish scene was new to them so they were learning a lot although their main interest was in Eastern Europe. I was a stranger and they took me in, I have an idea they were still on their Honeymoon. It was quite something for them to take me in to share their apartment when I was a complete stranger to them. I had a bunk in their dining room which was a kind of bookcase cum wardrobe. It was good to have somewhere to put my head down and the fellowship was sweet in the Lord. Ellen fed me at unusual hours as we never quite knew when we would arrive back from witnessing, it was never early. She really did look after me very well indeed. Next morning the centre was open for people to borrow books and drop in to chat about the Lord. I was thrilled to see so many coming and found it so easy to speak with the Russian Jews about the Lord.

That day I was to go to look for the Italian customs clearance station. Danny gave me directions as to how to find the address I had been given over the phone. Frank had quickly told me on the phone from Dover that I should look for an agent called Guiseippi Gruber at Via Enna, Aprilis, Rome. There a lady called Mrs. Bredow would try to help us. Danny located Via Enna on the map and gave me a few directions, and I set off into the city of Rome to look for the place. As I began to approach the city I started to feel more and more uneasy about the address. Surely they would not direct large transport lorries into the chaotic traffic of the city centre. With this in mind I decided to pull over and ask at a petrol station for some information. The young man there could not speak English but when I showed him the address, he shook his head and said, "Aprilia no Aprilis."

He pointed me towards the autostrada and kept saying "Aprilia, Aprilia."

I drove on to the autostrada but when I had driven about twenty miles I turned back thinking I must surely be on the wrong road, but that young man had seemed so sure, maybe he was right, so I duly turned back yet again. After driving for what seemed like a long way I saw a sign for Aprilia and followed the signs until I came to a town. How could I now find Gruber's office, if indeed this was were they were located. I decided to go to the local police station and ask for help. After looking around for a while I found the Carabineiri post and went inside. I was impressed by the spotlessly clean interior and the meticulously uniformed guards. They were most helpful and found the telephone number of Guiseppi Gruber for me. It was not possible for me to phone from the Carabineiri station so I went to a nearby coffee shop and borrowed a getoni (telephone token) for the coin operated telephone. When I got through to Grubers they were able to tell me that I was only about three minutes drive away from their office!

The office of the Guiseppi Gruber Transport company is located inside the customs compound at Aprilia on the top floor of the building. When I reached the place I went upstairs and asked for Mrs. Bredow. I explained why I was there and she invited me to come into the office and take a seat, I would be dealt with in a few minutes. It was now mid-morning and the office was busy with lorry drivers coming and going every few minutes. I waited as patiently as I could but after about two hours I was told that it was nearly lunch time and I should go away and return about three pm. I returned after lunch and took my seat again and there I remained until it was time for the office to close for the night. My papers had been looked at and taken to the Customs on the floor below, but nothing seemed to be happening. As they prepared to close up the office for the night I was told to come back in the morning. I left feeling that the only thing I had accomplished for that whole day was to locate the office.

Getting back to Ladispoli was easier for by now I was getting the hang of Italian style driving and beginning to feel less tense in the cut and thrust competition for space on the road. I finally made it back to Ladispoli where I walked about in the park like 'Alley' of trees where the Jews were selling things. I was able to chat to some of the people and make some acquaintances. Later that evening in Ladispoli there was a meeting which was attended by several hundred Russian Jews. Joel showed them a Christian film and preached the Gospel.

After the meeting a few of us were planning to go to deliver foodstuffs to some needy families. Just as we were starting to drive away from the meeting place Pastor Joel's wife rushed up to the mini-bus and told me that I was wanted to stand by the phone at the centre. The drivers had been on the phone to say that the lorry had already arrived in Italy and was at the end of the Autostrada loop near Rome. The drivers were waiting for my instructions about where to go next. I rushed over to the centre wondering how on earth I was going to be able to explain to them the way to Aprilia. Maybe I should drive to where they were and try to guide them, but while I could find my way back to Aprilia from Ladispoli I would have no idea how to get there from their location.

This could be very complicated indeed for the customs at Aprilia is really quite out of the way and difficult to find. As usual the Lord had His little 'raven' already prepared. Even before I reached the centre to await a further phone call from the men something truly wonderful happened. As Frank and his friend sat waiting in the lay-by another lorry pulled in beside them. The driver was from England and was glad to meet someone he could talk to. After a few minutes he asked Frank where our lorry was going to and he told him to the customs at Aprilis. The English driver told them that the name of the customs clearance station was APRILIA and that it was about forty miles to the South of Rome. He had actually just come from there and since it was his first time to make a customs clearance at Aprilia a friend had drawn him a map to guide him from the end of the autostrada loop. That map was drawn right from where our lorry was parked in the lay-by right to the gate of the customs station at Aprilia. Since the English driver had already been there he did not need his map any longer and gave it to our drivers.

When they phoned me a little later at the centre I could not under-stand at first how they could have found a map to the customs clearance station at Aprilia. Without any difficulty they reached Aprilia by fol-lowing the map and spent the night sleeping in the lorry in the customs compound. I promised that I would come first thing in the morning and try to get the clearance to import all the materials without payment of duty or further delay.

It was early next morning when Pastor Joel and I set off together in his car to make our way to Aprilia. How strange it seemed for me to be giving directions to him about where exactly to go in Italy. He kept on saying to me, "I am amazed that you found this place on your own." Of course I could never have found my way to Aprilia on my own, I am sure that the Lord was guiding and directing all the way. Driving along we had a good chance to talk about the work and share in fellowship. This dear brother had been so busy, with lines of people standing waiting to speak to him after all the meetings. We actually had very little opportunity up to this time to speak to each other. It was good now to have this chance to talk to each other and for me to hear his stories of so many lives changed by the power of the Gospel.

As we turned into the customs compound from the narrow street called Via Enna in the town of Aprilia what a welcome sight it was for my eyes to see the blue and white lorry. There it was parked in the long line of vehicles, I could make out the words Chart Hire and Belfast on the cab door. The men were really here, the Russian Bibles had actually arrived in Italy, there had been no mishap along the way. I rather hoped that now the lorry was here it would only take a few minutes to finalise the paperwork and we would soon be on our way............. But this was ITALY.

While the drivers went off to have a shower and freshen up we went to the office of Guiseppi Gruber on the top floor of the Customs building. There Mrs. Bredow greeted me like an old friend as we presented all our papers. These were passed on to a man who took them down stairs into the customs office. We were told to wait and after a while a man came and said we should really have gone to a different customs clearance station at Rome as the material was destined for Ladispoli. We explained that Ladispoli was only one centre and that the material would be distributed in seven or eight different centres. The customs again went into a huddle to discuss everything and an inspector went to examine the lorry. They seemed interested in the porridge bags until a bag was opened and Mike ate a handful of the meal to show them it really was only porridge. The biscuits too needed to be examined by a sanitary inspector for some reason. This all took quite some time and we were told to sit in an office while we waited for the customs to decide our fate. The pastor went out after a while to speak with them and when he returned he gave us a nasty shock. The first words he said to me were, "Ronnie, you better call a Prayer Meeting right away." I wondered what could be wrong and felt the cold hand of fear grip my heart.

Surely after coming all this way they were not going to refuse us entry. Surely after all the Lord had done we could not fall at this last hurdle? Surely we were not going be sent back without being able to deliver our goods? Pastor Joel explained that the Italian customs officials had decided to call a national STRIKE to start that very day. They were in no mood to clear anyone that morning for they were closing every post at lunchtime and would likely be out on strike for a week. I have no idea what the dispute was about or what were the rights and wrongs of it but there was one thing I knew for sure. I did not want that lorry stranded for a week at Aprilia.

I could not stay for an extra week and I was afraid if we were not there the goods might never reach the Russian Jews. It would be a case of so near and yet so far, for the lorry might be stranded at Aprilia until it was too late to reach them. People were arriving daily but others were leaving daily too for the United States. Politicians were talking about closing the route through Italy which would mean no further arrivals of Russian Jews once those in transit reached the centres. This unique opportunity would pass in a few months when those people who were already there and those still arriving would be processed. Every day was vital and any delay would mean some souls passing beyond our reach without having received the Bible. So we did indeed call a prayer meeting. I expect that it is the only time that a prayer meeting has ever been held at the customs post in Aprilia, but pray we certainly did. We sat on our chairs in a little huddle and prayed one by one. One brother prayed and I remember so clearly some of his words. "Lord I ask you to release this precious cargo of your Word without any further delay."

After we had spent some time in prayer I decided to put feet to our prayers and go and talk to someone, so as the brethren continued to seek the Lord I went outside. As I began to descend the stairway I met the little Italian customs agent who we had seen in Grubers and some conversation followed. "What is your name?" I asked him. He told me that his name was Claudio Avitabile. I said to him, "Claudio, I am Ronnie McCracken and I come from Ireland........ " At this his face lit up and he told me that he loved Ireland, his wife was from Waterford and every year he liked to come for his holidays. Ireland for him was so green and so cool and he loved the rain. I remember saying to him, "Claudio! Ireland is not going to love you if we don't get that lorry out of here very soon. The Christian people in Northern Ireland have given all these things to help the Russian refugees and will not be very happy if they are held up for a week." As Italy was looking forward to being host nation for the World cup football that June I mentioned that bad publicity for Italy would not be nice at this time. Claudio told me to go into the office and wait for a few minutes more while he would see what could be done.

In about ten minutes time he came in with all our papers stamped by the Italian Customs. Claudio was a lovely little Italian 'raven' who the Lord had prepared to help us, right down to him having an Irish wife. When I asked Claudio what would be the amount of the bill for Guiseppe Gruber for their services as customs clearance agents he said that there would be no bill. Their services would be donated free to help the cause as we were serving God.

Praise the Lord we were cleared to import all the material without payment of a single penny of duty to the Italian government or even having to pay the agent. All those thousands of Bibles and all that Gospel literature would shortly be available to the Russian Jews. I noted the time as we finalised the last details with the Custodians of Finance, it was exactly one twenty pm. Italian time. At one thirty pm. all the customs posts were closed as the customs started the strike and no transports could move in or out of Italy during the next days. We did not fully realise the extent of the victory God had given us in answer to prayer that day until later on.

How my heart rejoiced when we reached Ladispoli with the lorry. As we threw open the doors to commence unloading the cargo a number of people arrived to help us. Among them were Pavel, and his father Paul and several other Russian Jews. What a sight it was to see Russian Jews carrying thousands of Bibles and Gospel of Mark newspapers into the rented store. Backwards and forwards they tramped up and down a very steep ramp for the store was an underground garage. They carried all the material out of the truck just as our 'ravens' in Ireland had carried it on. The only difference this time was that these were Russian 'ravens'. It wasn't long before we were all feeling the strain and the perspiration was flowing freely. The pastor worked as hard as anybody and we enjoyed wonderful fellowship as we toiled in this happy task. I had stopped for a breather by the tail-board of the truck when Pavel came up to me. The words that young Russian spoke to me made the whole effort worthwhile and I shall never forget them as long as I live. Pavel took my hand and said, "Thank you for this beautiful thing you have done in bringing the Word of God to our people."

Yes it was a wonderful thing but I did not do it. It was the Lord's doing, entirely His. He merely allowed me the unspeakable privilege to have a share in what He was doing. The Lord does not need any one of us to do His work. He can carry it on without us and He does. Often we only get in His way by our failure to recognise what He wants to do, but sometimes it is our privilege to share in it and to see what the Lord is doing. He commanded the 'ravens' all along the way, He supplied all the needs, He opened all the borders, He manipulated all the officials. HE IS THE LORD. Blessed be His Name.

One evening the Lord reminded me that this was all His doing when He said to me, "I am not doing all this for you, or even for your Mission, I am doing it for MY PEOPLE ISRAEL." The Lord had promised long ago that one day He would bring them out from the north country and gather them from the coasts of the earth. He had spoken through the Hebrew prophets and declared that one day there would be an exodus from the north country that would surpass even the Exodus from Egypt. Jeremiah chapter 23 verse 7 says, "Therefore behold, the days come, saith the Lord, that they shall no more say, The Lord liveth which brought up the children of Israel out of the land of Egypt; But, The Lord liveth which brought up and which led out the seed of the house of Israel out of the north country....." There can be no doubt that Russia is to the north and now God was bringing about an amazing exodus of Jews from that land. The thousands passing through Italy were only a small part of the vast movement of people taking place. Every day special flights were landing at Tel-Aviv's Ben Gurion airport. During only one month (July 1990) no less than SIXTEEN THOUSAND RUSSIAN JEWS arrived in Israel. Yes the Lord is fulfilling His word and bringing to pass the things He promised so long ago.

After we had unloaded all the materials that had been so lovingly donated and the Bibles that had been so wonderfully provided there was time for a little rest. When Frank and Mike had freshened up I took them to the square in Ladispoli so that they could see for themselves what was happening. They too were moved as they saw the crowds of Russian Jews milling around. We walked through the little park like alley where the people were trying to sell their bits and pieces. Every time I walked there I was filled with compassion for these poor people. The trauma of having to leave homeland and friends was bad enough but to have to leave behind everything you had worked all your life for was something else. Many of these people were university graduates and very highly qualified. I spoke to Mathematicians, Engineers, Cardiologists, and specialists in Oncology to name but a few. Now they were standing in this little park which they called "the Alley" trying to sell whatever they had to obtain a little money. We did purchase a few small Russian souvenirs to have as reminders of the people.

Later that evening we drove to a town about thirty miles to the south of Rome where a large number of Russian Jews were waiting in transit. The team arrived in the mini bus and went to a huge car parking area, this was where the post would be distributed so the Jews would gather there later on. When we arrived, there were already quite a number of people around and once again there was a small market with the same Russian goods for sale. An announcement was made that in about an hour we would begin to distribute the Bible. The word was soon spread and the people began to gather in large numbers. As the darkness began to deepen the car park became crowded and the night air was filled with the sounds of Russian words all around us.

Brother Joel came to me and said, "Since you are the man who brought the Bibles I think that you should be the one to hand them out." I wanted Frank and Mike to have the experience of helping to give out the Bibles they had so willingly transported so we finally agreed that the three men from Northern Ireland would distribute the Scriptures. Joel told me to be prepared for things to get rough but I could hardly imagine that it could be rough handing out Bibles. Still even with the words of warning we were not prepared for what happened next. The back doors of the minibus were opened and an old trestle table set up across them and we three positioned ourselves behind the table. We set two or three boxes of Bibles out on the table and imagined that the people would come quietly and orderly to receive a copy from us. We had only opened the first package and given out the first few Bibles when the realisation dawned on the Russian Jews that we really did have quantities of Bibles. There was a noise as the word passed through the crowd and then a surge of people pressed on us, the table was pushed sideways and Mike was pushed into the mini bus as hands reached out from all directions. Some reached in through the opening between the doors and body of the mini bus and other hands came under the doors to tap at our legs in an effort to attract attention. The doors of the mini bus were bent out of shape and required a lot of persuasion later on to close. As the people pressed in on us we did not so much give the Bibles to them, they took them from us. That one evening we distributed ONE THOUSAND copies of the whole Bible and many copies of our Gospel of Mark newspapers as well as New Testaments and booklets. It was late in the night when we finally finished our work and all we had left were the empty cartons. I deliberately walked around the car park looking everywhere to see if there were any pieces of our literature thrown away. Even though I looked everywhere I could not find even one page or booklet that had been discarded. These people were so glad to receive the message of God that they treasured it.

We had tried to confine the people to one copy for a family and I remember one man walking away with two Bibles under his arm. When I asked why he had taken two he replied that he had family in the Soviet Union and was anxious to try and post a Bible to them. Of course we rejoiced to think that a Jewish family in Russia could receive the Scriptures in this way and we assured him that he was welcome to take two Bibles for this purpose.

That evening we had taken with us two cartons filled with the illustrated books designed for the children. While these were printed with children in mind they also proved to be in great demand among the adults. Our instructions had been that we should distribute one carton at the car park and keep one back for another place which we would call at on our way back to Ladispoli. However when we had distributed our quota there were still people coming and asking for more. One lady came and pleaded with me so earnestly saying that she would need one for her child. Even though I assured her that we had no more to distribute there that night she still pleaded for a book for her child. How could I stand there and say to her that we could not give her one when I knew that there was a full box under the seat. In response to her pleading I took out the second carton and opened it intending to take out only one book for this lady and put it away again. As she received her copy others pressed in with children by the hand pleading for books, it took less than five minutes for the carton to be emptied. In less time than it takes to read this they were all gone and yet still the people came, reaching out in hope. Another lady came rushing up to us and began to intercede for a book for her child. "I would need one for my child, I want my child to learn about God. Do you have one for me?" When we told her that they were all gone she refused to accept that we had none. To satisfy her Mike and I had to search through all the empty cartons to demonstrate that there were really none left. Then she asked, "Will you come back tomorrow?" Alas there was no way we could return the next day and indeed I was never able to return there at all. It was her earnest plea that touched a chord in my heart. I needed to supply more of these books for the children and adults. That was when the idea to return with a second lorry began to take shape in my mind. If I could get more literature from the Slavic Gospel Association press in Marpent on the French-Belgian border we could meet the need. Much more was to happen before we would be on the road to Marpent again.

When we returned that evening to Ladispoli I took Frank and Mike to meet two people who had made a deep impression on me. They were a mother and son who I had met in remarkable circumstances. During my first visit to Italy I had been walking in the market place and stopped to speak to some Russian Jews. A young man of sixteen was trying to sell a shawl in the market that day but had decided that he was not being very successful. We fell into conversation and he asked me if I would like to go to his apartment to meet his mother. He explained that she was a teacher of English and that she could talk to me much better than he could. As we had set off along the street together, I had no idea where we were going and I wondered if I was wise to go off with him. When we arrived at the apartment his mother welcomed me warmly and we talked for a while. During our conversation she explained that she was not religious and did not believe, I said that did not matter I would pray for her anyway that she would soon get her visa to go America. After a while she asked me if I would like to have some tea and she began to set about making it. The tea leaves were placed in a pot and a little hot water added and the whole thing was covered up with a cloth and set aside for quite some time, then the pot was filled up with boiling hot water and we had super strong tea that would have done justice to any building site. As we sat sipping the strong black tea from our glasses I was trying to hold the scalding glass by my fingertips. The lady explained to me that she was very sorry that she could not offer me any biscuit or cake as she did not have any. On the sideboard nearby was a can of fish that looked like sardines. The metal was rolled back and half of the fish had been consumed, it seemed like they had eaten half for lunch and would use the rest for dinner.

Next day I went to the super market and purchased as much as I could for them, Russian tastes are different from ours as they have not been used to many of the things we are so familiar with. I thought that lots of fresh fruit would be good for them and even managed to get some strawberries. After I had delivered the groceries to them as I prepared to leave the lady brought me the shawl and explained to me that her son could not succeed to sell it and that she was ashamed to try to sell things in a public place, I could take it for my wife and maybe she would like it. It was a cream coloured shawl with brightly coloured roses printed on it and looked very typically Russian. It was kind of them to give it to me for Pat, but even as I took it an idea began to form in my mind. It was not the type of garment I could visualise my wife wearing to church on a Sunday morning! It would only be stored away in a drawer somewhere. On the other hand I could make use of it as a reminder to people to pray for this family and all the other Russian Jews both in and out of Russia.

I would make a little bookmark with some scripture texts on and place a portion of the shawl as a reminder of the Russians. My friends could then have a bookmark with something that actually came out of Russia with one of these people whom the Lord was miraculously bringing from the North country. Hopefully it would serve as a reminder to people to pray and it would also to help them to understand that God was wonderfully fulfilling His Word. Those who wished to give something for the bookmarks could do so and the money for this would go directly to that family to help them start a new life. The printer who I engaged to print the bookmarks turned out to be a Roman Catholic but when I told him what I wanted he did the job in record time and when I asked for the bill he refused to accept any payment.

I wanted Frank and Mike to meet these people and so that night we called at the apartment on Via Odescalci and rang the bell. When we entered the apartment block and started to climb the stairs our friends were waiting at the top, the lady was literally jumping up and down and could not wait to tell us her news. Only that day she had received the information that their visas were granted and they would leave on February 14 for America. As she told us the words rushed out spilling over one another but in the midst of it all I could hear her say, "Your God must have played some kind of trick on me to get me the visa so fast, you must have asked your friends to pray." Yes lots of friends were praying daily, those little bookmarks were reminding the Lord's people to pray and prayer was being answered. While many had to wait more than ten months for a visa our friends received theirs faster than any others in their group. When I placed into their hands the money from the bookmarks they at first refused to take it. I had to explain that it was theirs, they had tried without success to sell the shawl so I had kind of acted on their behalf and 'sold' it to my friends, they would have to take the money as it did not belong to me and I could not keep it. I was able to give them the equivalent of what was then 9,000 roubles which was more than they had ever seen in their lives. There were many tears of gratitude and they simply could not understand why anyone would show them so much love. The lady kept saying, "I don't know how to react to this, no one has ever done us such kindness in all our lives. We have experienced hatred and scorn but never love like this." Frank and Mike had to drink some Russian tea and we had a good time of chatting about what the future might hold. These friends shared with us that they had mixed feelings about America, they wanted to go but at the same time they were afraid of what they would meet there. We tried to reassure them and encourage them before we left that evening. I saw them once more before they left Italy. It was an unspeakable privilege to be able to assist them and to feel that the Lord was declaring an interest in their lives. At three am. on February 14 they left Ladispoli square to begin the long journey to America and are now striving to adjust to the new culture and lifestyle there in San Diego.

Now that our drivers had seen and felt the reality of the work for themselves they were anxious to get home to Northern Ireland. They would leave next morning and should be home about a week before me. I carefully checked the list of people I wanted them to telephone on their arrival. These interested friends would have been praying for the safe arrival of the goods and I wanted them to know that the Lord had indeed answered prayer. When Frank and Mike set off I waved them goodbye and prayed for their safety on the roads through Italy and France. Little did I imagine that it would be more than a week before they would reach home or that I would be back in Northern Ireland before them. The Italian customs men were still on strike and the border was closed. When our men approached the border there was a line of trucks and lorries about seven miles long stretching from the platform at Mont Blanc right back down the road. It was impossible to move and they had to wait there in the snowy alps until the strike was settled. The Italian Red Cross had to bring hot coffee and food to the many stranded drivers. The victory God gave us when we prayed at Aprilia was all the more tremendous when we realised that the Lord brought the lorry into Italy fully loaded but we couldn't get it out again empty.

All this took extra time yet when I asked Frank for the bills for the lorry hire, the road tolls and the Mont Blanc Tunnel passage this is what he said. "The Lord only told me to move the stuff for you, He did not tell me to charge you. When the Lord tells me to ask you for money then that is when I will ask for it. He has not told me to ask for it so there is no bill." What a tremendous contribution Frank made to this effort, he freely gave his time and actually travelled at his own expense to get the Word of Life to people who in the main had never seen a Bible in their entire lives. The Russian Jews like millions of others in the Soviet Union, had been brought up under a militant atheistic system that had made it almost impossible to learn about God. Christians have suffered greatly but have been helped by the fact that they had a living faith and a personal Saviour. Believers in the West, often at great risk, had taken help to their brothers and sisters. The Jews did not have so much

With Dr. Boris Nicolaevitch Kidney Specialist of Hospital 26.

Two Kidney Dialysis Machines in our home.

Tearful Farewells from Russian Children.

From Seattle to Seven Mile Straight
Dr. Chris Blagg's Kidney Machine arrives.

Russian Jews Reading the Gospel of Mark.

Our present van which is used for local collections.

With Jewish friends at Kiev Airport.

Enjoying lunch at Ballycraigy Church.

"I've Got Mine!" loaded down with gifts.

Pictured with Pastor & Mrs Wang, Ming Tao who
suffered at the hands of the Communists.

Mrs. Natasha Tonkonogy who interpreted for us.

The late Inspector Gordon Peters. (R.U.C.)

help from outside and since they do not have a living Saviour to sustain them they fared much worse in the Soviet Union than Evangelical Believers. A few places had open synagogues, and one or two even had clandestine Hebrew classes but most had nothing. Jewish life was not possible for the vast majority of Russian Jews.

After the men had left Ladispoli I had an appointment to keep that was to be a very wonderful experience. I was to give the message at the meeting next morning and I needed to meet with the interpreter to discuss things. It had been advertised that I would give a talk on the subject 'The Greatest Jewish Singer and Poet of all Time.' I was of course going to attempt to preach about David the Psalmist of Israel. The man who had been doing the interpretation had just gone to America and a lady had offered to take over, the only difficulty was that she did not know anything about the Bible or spiritual things. It was all brand new to her and we would need to do a lot of preparation together if things were going to go well. Natasha came to Danny and Ellen's apartment that morning and we sat in the kitchen trying to prepare for the meeting. We had Russian Bibles and English Bibles and dictionaries and notebooks piled up on the table. As we began to discuss what would happen at the meeting Natasha confided in me that she was very nervous and did not want to stand up in front of all the people and look foolish if she made mistakes. I told her not to worry, that I would explain to the people that since I came from Northern Ireland my English was rather different and that if there were any difficulties the people should blame my accent and not her interpretation. When I realised that she was really worried about the meeting I suggested that we should pray and ask the Lord for His help in this matter.

I would pray that she would be helped with the interpretation and that I would be helped as to what I should say. Before we prayed I asked her if there was anything else she was worried about and she confided in me that she was anxious about the situation regarding her family getting visas for Canada. So I began to pray that the Lord would give us all the help we would need and to ask Him to open the way in His time for the family to move on to Canada. As I prayed I ventured a quick glance at Natasha to see how she was reacting to the prayer, she was looking around the little kitchen and seemed amazed, who could I be talking to? There was no one else there except we two. After the prayer I asked

Natasha if she knew who David was and I was delighted when she said, "Of course I know who David is," but my delight was short lived for she went on to say, "He is my husband." Natasha did not know about David the one time King of Israel or about his psalms. The fact that all this was new to her made our task all the more difficult, many of the words I wanted to use were not in her vocabulary and had to be researched in the dictionary.

I was going to give a message based on a trilogy of Psalms. 22, 23 and 24. In Psalm 22 we have a picture of the Cross of Christ which I called, 'The Crucified Saviour and His Cross', while in Psalm 23 we have, 'The Comforting Shepherd and His Crook'.   In Psalm 24 we see 'The Coming Sovereign and His Crown'. In Psalm 22 we find the amazing picture of our Crucified Lord with His hands pierced, His garments gambled over and enclosed by the assembly of the wicked. It is such a graphic picture made all the more remarkable by the fact that it was written so long ago. Over one thousand five hundred years before anyone had been put to death by crucifixion David described it in such amazing detail. The Jews never ever practised this form of capital punishment at any time in their history. They stoned criminals to death in a much more humane manner by dropping a single large stone on the offenders head and chest. Crucifixion was devised in ancient Carthage and taken up by the Romans.

How could David the Jewish King of Israel describe so clearly the Death of Christ? How could a Jew know anything about it all those years before it happened? The answer is he could NOT have known anything about it UNLESS the Holy Spirit gave him a revelation. Surely here is the clearest evidence that what happened to Jesus was not just by chance or an accident of history. It was not something which the Jews are responsible for, Almighty God had ordered it and caused His servants to predict it by prophecy hundreds of years before it became a fact. David was able to describe the death of Christ as clearly as if he was present standing at the Cross. Now as we worked our way through the message it seemed to me as if I could see a light coming on in Natasha's soul. It was almost tangible as the illumination of the Holy Spirit seemed to fill her. Next morning the meeting place was filled to standing room with Russian Jews and after a few brief introductions I was asked to speak to the assembled people. Natasha and I took our places at the front of the hall and we began to address the people. I say we because without this Russian Jewish lady there was no way I could have spoken. In her own special way Natasha was another of God's 'ravens' sent to meet a particular need at that time. Before we began to deliver the message I decided to tell the people something about what had happened to me in the Soviet Union years ago.

It was away back in 1974 that my friend Gordon Peters and I went to Russia to bring some help to the Christians. Gordon was a member of the security forces in Northern Ireland and a keen Christian. He decided to accompany me on a mission to bring Bibles to some Christians inside Russia during a very difficult period. Unfortunately for us we were arrested not long after crossing the Finnish border and detained for a time. We were kept in separate rooms and subjected to interrogation at least five times. We were stripped of our clothes and I was kicked and punched for destroying a piece of paper containing some names and addresses. Eventually we were deported to Finland minus my almost new Peugeot car which was seized by the Russians along with all my money. The official documents declared that we had been found guilty of smuggling arms, explosives, narcotics and poisonous material. We were found guilty of breaking article number 78 of the Russian Criminal code. The penalty for this offence was ten years in prison followed with five years in exile with the confiscation of all ones goods. The Soviet authorities decided to be lenient and only confiscate our property. The biggest problem we had was that when we arrived on the Finnish border in a Soviet refrigerated lorry the Finnish guards almost believed we were guilty. The fact that we came from Northern Ireland seemed to make them think that we might just be interested in such kinds of materials as arms and explosives. The Finnish police gave us a nights free accommodation in the Helsinki lock up. I remember how very confused we felt at the 'failure' of our mission, the many times we asked ourselves why. We had prayed so earnestly for the Lord to bring us through, had He not answered? Then there was the loss of the car and all our things, that was a bitter blow which I certainly could not afford.

Now all these years later here I was relating this incident to hundreds of Jews from Russia in this old theatre in Italy. As I spoke and Natasha translated something amazing happened , all over the audience

I could see tears glinting in eyes. There a man wiped his hand across his cheek, here a Babushka (Russian Grandmother) dabbed at her eye with a handkerchief. A stillness crept over the crowd and they listened with rapt attention as I went on to preach from the Word of God.

As our meeting drew to a close with a challenge to the people to trust in the Lord as their Messiah and Saviour, the entire congregation stood to their feet and began to applaud. I was so surprised as this is something I am not used to, here were hundreds of Jews applauding me because I had told them that they needed God's Salvation. As the meeting concluded some of those who were moving on to America spoke warm words of appreciation for the help they had received while others testified to having come to know the Lord in Italy. Our meeting finished around about twelve noon that Sunday but it was almost five thirty pm. before I managed to get any lunch. At the close of the meeting so many people were waiting to talk to us about the things of God. One after another came up and expressed their sympathy that I should have had to go through such an experience in Russia but added, "You can understand us, you can feel what our life has been." Suddenly I began to understand that there was indeed a purpose in what had happened to us so long ago. God had been preparing us for this day, our sad experience in Russia was now being used by the Lord to win the hearts of these people. Mr. Rabinovitch, the Russian border guard who arrested us (he was a Jew himself) was really only one of God's 'ravens' sent years in advance to prepare the way. The Lord used that experience to give us favour with the people and to draw some to Himself, after all those long years. Truly the ways of the Lord are past finding out.

After bidding my many friends farewell I returned to Ireland once again but with plans to get back to Italy with more material as soon as possible. As soon as I arrived home I set in motion some new ideas that had formulated in my mind. I had obtained a book entitled 'Let the Rabbis speak', which was an account of the salvation of twelve Rabbis. This could be useful to give to the small percentage of religious Jews we were encountering, they too needed to hear the Gospel message. The work of printing this book was undertaken by Central Printers of Bangor who turned out two thousand copies of this book in Russian in record quick time. The ink was still drying when they were collected from Bangor. Another idea I had was to record the entire text of Mark's

Gospel on to cassettes and give them out on a loan basis. People could then listen to the English pronunciation as well as read the text. This would help the people who were trying to learn English and they would be getting the Word through hearing as well as reading. Mr. David Winter spent a full week reading the text on to tape to get it word perfect. The only trouble was that it was too long to fit on to one cassette and I could foresee problems with having to use two. It could cause confusion if the people started with the second cassette by mistake and the words did not seem to agree. Olivet Recording Studios had the answer to this problem, Roy Rainey made hundreds of special length cassettes and we were able to get the whole of Mark's Gospel onto one cassette. Olivet made over five hundred copies of these and delivered them to my home. When I asked how much I owed for the work and the materials I was told that there was no bill, in fact Roy proceeded to hand me a cheque from Olivet Recordings to assist us in delivering the cassettes to Italy! How very grateful we are for all the hard work carried out and the kindness shown. I was specially pleased when I learned that the recording tape used was manufactured in Israel near to the Sea of Galilee. It seemed to add something to the wonder of what the Lord was doing, the fact that the very tape came from the land He lived in and from the Galilee He loved so well. Roy Rainey was Roy 'raven' that day without a doubt. Another five hundred English Bibles were purchased from Faith Mission in Belfast for some of our English speaking contacts and then we were ready to set off again to Italy. This time I would fly to Paris and pick up a lorry from a hire company and drive to Marpent on the Belgian border. Mr. Trevor Eves, of the Bangor Worldwide Missionary Convention, and Mr. Gordon Campbell would drive from Northern Ireland with the books and cassettes and meet me at Marpent where we would load up the lorry with thousands more copies of the illustrated Life of Christ books for the children. I left the men to collect the cassettes and books and took my flight to Paris.

I had made a booking through Avis Rent-A-Car and fully expected that a small lorry would be waiting for me at Charles De Gaulle airport when I arrived. However Avis had got things confused and I arrived to find that they had a Mercedes limousine waiting for me! I managed to convince them that I really wanted a lorry and they began to search all of Paris for a vehicle. At last they found one and sent me to a suburb of

Paris to collect it.   My heart sank when I saw the vehicle they had for me, it was really terrible, in very poor condition and dirty.   It was all they had so I had to make it do for there was no way I could carry my cargo in a limousine.   The engine had a serious oil leak and I had to keep topping it up with oil all the time.   The oil sprayed out everywhere and before long I was looking like a mechanic.   I had been planning to go to Stuttgart to collect some other Russian literature but decided that I better not risk the extra journey. I drove to Marpent and next morning Gordon and Trevor arrived, they had been travelling all night and were not the brightest when I met them. Bill Kapitaniuk did a quick calculation and decided that I could probably carry about six thousand of his books on the lorry.   We loaded the books on but there was still space so I asked if they had any more ready.   When they said that there were I asked them to put on another thousand, then we loaded another thousand and the springs groaned. I was thinking about all those children and I was anxious to give as many of them as possible the story of Jesus.   I looked at Bill and said "Please put another thousand books on the lorry."   Bill was a bit doubtful and Gordon said, "Do you want me to run behind?" The tyres bulged a bit as the last of the nine thousand books were loaded on to the old vehicle and I closed the doors. The books Trevor and Gordon had brought from Bangor were already on board as were the cassettes. The old lorry groaned and rattled and sprayed oil everywhere but it got us over the Alps and into Italy. I drove all the way to Ladispoli and we arrived there at four in the morning. I did not want to wake up the friends at this unearthly hour so I decided that I would scale the wall into the storeroom and Gordon would pass the parcels over to me. It took me about ten minutes to climb the wall and unlock the inner door and when I was ready I called for Gordon to begin passing the packages over to me. There was no response to my calls and whistles so I had to climb back over the wall to see what on earth was wrong. There was nothing wrong except that my helper was slumped in the cab fast asleep and no amount of banging on the window could wake him up. He was so tired that when the engine switched off he switched off too. I had to wake my friends to get the key for the gate and I unloaded the packages while Gordon slept like a baby in the front of the lorry.

I managed to get a couple of hours sleep before going once more to Aprilia to finalise the customs papers once again. That night we held a meeting where we showed 'The Hiding Place.' It was in English so Pavel had to interpret the sound. He was Corrie and Casper and the Germans and everyone else as well. The problem was he could not keep up with the film so the whole thing was out of synchronisation. It did not seem to matter to the Russian Jews who still came in their hundreds to watch. Once again it was precious to see some people wait to put their trust in the Messiah. We had to leave next day and drive back to Paris to return the lorry and I was glad when I was able to hand in the keys.

I made one final visit to Italy for a special reason. Pat had endured our home being turned into a warehouse and had supported me in everything I was doing so I wanted her to see something of the work before it finally ceased. Together we returned to Italy for a few days, it was lovely to be there again. We had a very special Sunday meeting in Ladispoli and afterwards spent the afternoon with Natasha, David and Anya at Pastor Joel's home. That was a very precious day we will never forget. Next day Pat was able to assist in the distribution of food and helped to give out some Speedicook Oats that had been in our home. The Russian Jews came with their special ration cards and had them stamped as they collected the aid we had for them, they left with loving words about the Messiah ringing in their ears. As we worked that last day Pat drew my attention to a little Russian Jewish boy who was running across the courtyard. He was wearing a Tee shirt with a big green shamrock on it and the word Ireland emblazoned across his tummy. That shirt had come from our lorry, it had been in our home, some kind 'raven' had sent it to us. Suddenly it came to us both at the same moment; the words which our Saviour spoke so long ago, "Inasmuch as ye have done it unto one of the least of these MY BRETHREN ye have done it unto me."

The crowds of Russian Jews have gone from Ladispoli now and the other seven towns they were staying in. The camp has returned to its former use as a centre for summer holidays. The apartments where our friends found temporary shelter have other occupants now and the sound of Russian has disappeared from the streets and markets. Natasha and David have started a new life in Canada. Pavel has gone to Pensylvania with his parents. Sam, Slava, Yevgeny, Eugene, Yefim, Ludmilla, Sergei, Benjamin, Michael and all the rest are gone and perhaps I will never see them again on this scene of time. They are all very special people for me and I will never forget them.

Natasha wrote from Edmonton and said, "I felt in Italy that I was part of something great that the Lord was doing when I stood up in front of the people to interpret the wonderful words; perhaps nothing of the kind will ever happen in my life again."

Yes it was something special and unique and none of us may ever see something like it again. The amazing exodus of Jews from Russia, the miraculous provision for thousands of Bibles, the wonderful way the Lord provided all the necessary funds, the porridge, clothes, sweets and blankets. It was all so special and extraordinary that surely it could never be repeated. And yet again............ who knows what will be, for as the title of this book says:

God's Ravens still fly.

~ PART TWO ~

We had been standing one evening in the car park at Anzio after distributing Bibles and other Christian literature to the Russian Jews when Pavel Lebedev approached me. He looked deep into my eyes and as he took my hand repeated some words he had spoken to me earlier in Ladispoli. It seems as if I can still hear his voice and still see his expression. His eyes were intense and he had almost the look of an Old Testament prophet with his neat well trimmed beard. "Ronnie, I want to thank you for the beautiful thing you have done in bringing the Word of God to our people, we never had it before. But Ronnie, what about the people who will never leave Russia? What about the old and the sick, the Gentiles as well as the Jews? Could you not do something to help them?" Pavel had escaped from the Soviet Union but he was concerned about those still left behind. That night he laid a burden on my shoulders which has remained until this day. I think that if I had realised even in part what it was going to mean I would probably have run about a thousand miles away. That night the Lord used Pavel's words to place a responsibility on my shoulders which has been extremely heavy at times. Faith has been challenged again and again. The amount of physical labour that was waiting for me and my helpers we could not imagine. It was just as well that the Lord hid it from me. Pavel was soon on his way to the United States where he has made a new life in Pensylvania but his words live with me constantly. I could not escape from them. I would have to return to Russia and see if there was a way to reach out to the needy, the elderly, the sick and the poor.

CHAPTER NINE

Return to the Soviet Union

A short time after arriving home from the final trip to Italy I received a letter from Russia. It came from the city that was then still called Lenningrad, from an old friend of mine. Many years earlier I met Sergei at the First Baptist Church in Leningrad and we had become friends. At that time he and three other young men were allowed to come out of the Soviet Union to study in London at Spurgeon's college and we had maintained our friendship over the years. Sergei had visited my home and I had arranged some meetings for him in Northern Ireland during the mid-seventies. One of our Sunday school children presented him with a Thompson Chain Reference Bible which he still uses to this day. Sergei had written to tell me that he had taken on a massive project. Under the new Gorbachev policies of Glasnost and Peristroika the authorities had decided to return a huge church building in Leningrad to a group of Believers. The building was wrecked and in ruins but there was a possibility to repair it and return it to the use for which it was originally intended, the worship of God. Sergei wondered if I would be able to help the small group of Christians there to get the project under way. I had not been to Russia for nearly ten years but it seemed that this was the time for me to return to see what the situation was now. I immediately went to the Russian Embassy in London and applied for a Visa which after all the years of refusals was granted.

I was told to join a group which would leave from Gatwick the following Friday evening. It was all arranged at very short notice and I expected that I would be joining a group of English tourists who were going to have a holiday in Russia.

To my surprise I discovered on arriving at Gatwick that the group consisted of several Americans, several South Africans and a couple from New Zealand. There was one Welshman and a young English communist who made up the group. I suppose that I should not have been surprised at the way the Lord arranged things but I was amazed when I discovered that many of the group members were Jewish people who were going to Russia to visit their relatives. The former Mayor of Durban was one of the Jewish members of our party with whom I struck up a particular friendship. For the next two weeks we travelled together and had a very interesting time.

Intourist Moscow Ltd. appointed us a guide called Marina who at times was somewhat overwhelmed by her task, so having had some experience with leading groups I volunteered to help her. Every day she gave me the microphone on the bus to let me speak to the people and every day I would tell them a few Irish jokes to make them laugh before speaking to them about the Lord. Sometimes after listening Marina would say to me, "I am not a Believer." We are still in touch from time to time and maybe one day she will become a real Believer.

The people I was travelling with soon became good friends and we really enjoyed a wonderful time. One evening just as I was about to go out of the hotel I met two Americans from our party in the lobby. They asked me if I knew a good restaurant where they could find food they would be able eat. I told them that my usual system in a strange place was to ask a taxi driver to take me to a good restaurant. The outcome of our conversation was that we went together to a Georgian cafe that our taxi driver recommended. The food proved to be truly awful but we had a good time together laughing and joking. During the course of the evening Barry asked me directly, "What do you do Ronnie, and why are you in Russia?" I explained to him that I am a Christian who has a special interest in the Jewish people and that I was seeking ways to bring them help. When I had finished my answer Barry and Francine looked at each other and then asked me, "Did you pick us out deliberately?" I was a little confused and reminded them that they had approached me in the lobby. I asked why they had suddenly decided to ask if I had picked them out and they explained that they were both Jewish. Barry and Francine where about the most Gentile looking Jews I had ever met. The Lord in His own wonderful way had placed us on the same tour and here we were having dinner together. It was good to be able to share with them the story of the Messiah of Israel.

On another day as I was leaving our hotel the New Zealand couple asked me where I was going. I told them I was on my way to visit an elderly Russian Christian lady who I been supporting for many years. They expressed a desire to come with me so that they could see inside a Russian apartment and I agreed to take them. We travelled together in a taxi to the home of Larissa Alexevna and as we drove along I mentioned that I would be reading the Bible and praying in the apartment when we arrived. These people were originally from Wales although they now lived in New Zealand. They told me that in their childhood they remembered their father reading from the Bible every night. When they saw the conditions in Larissa's home they were so moved that on our return they organised a collection of money from all the group members to help her. They gave me the money and an assortment of foodstuffs to take to Larissa. I was deeply touched when I saw what these people had done for this dear Christian soul. Every one of the group members gave generously to assist her including the former Mayor of Durban.

On another day as we were chatting one of the South African members of the group told me that he had been the leader of a dance band and played the saxophone. After we had some further conversation he told me he was going out for a while and asked if I would be willing to wait in the lobby to receive his Russian relatives in case they would arrive while he was away. True enough they did come early to the Moscow hotel where they were greeted by an Ulsterman! The South Africans were delighted to meet their cousin for the first time when they returned although they were a little shocked to discover that the lady he had married was a dwarf. It seemed that in the small village where he lived no woman would agree to marry him because he was Jewish, so he sent for a Jewish girl from another part of the country and when she arrived he discovered that she was a dwarf. Some months later I received a letter from South Africa containing a newspaper clipping which announced the death of this friend as a result of a terrible road accident.

His widow was in hospital with two broken arms but asked her son to write and let me know the terrible news.

Among my souvenirs of that trip I have a photograph of a South African dentist. He and his wife were members of the group and one Sunday I met them out walking in Red Square in Moscow. After some casual conversation I told them I was just out for a walk after attending the morning meeting at the Baptist Church and that I was going back for the afternoon service. They told me that they would love to visit a church in Russia and when I invited them to come along they decided that they would accompany me to the afternoon service. As we talked together on our way to the Baptist Church I discovered that Robbie's wife was already a Believer on the Lord Jesus Christ but that he was not. At the service in the church we had to stand as there were no vacant seats. Robbie was deeply touched by what he saw that day at the service. Some days later we visited a Russian Orthodox church and Robbie and I had a long talk about the Lord. Later on his wife said to me, "I don't know what you said to Robbie but he is a changed man." I was so delighted when I received a letter from South Africa a few months later telling me how Robbie had come to believe that Jesus is the only Saviour while he was in Russia. Robbie sent me the photograph which we had taken together in Red Square that Sunday, and I shall treasure it always.

It was during this time in Moscow that I went to meet my old friend Sergei at the office of the Baptist Church. While I stood outside waiting a man came out and asked if I was looking for someone. I explained that I was waiting for a friend from Leningrad and he asked me who that might be. When I said that it was Sergei he said, "I was a student in London with Sergei." I took a closer look but could not at first recognise the man. I enquired of him if he had been at Spurgeon's College and when he said yes I asked him if he remembered the graduation day when Sergei finished his studies. He was a little bit indignant and said he could not forget that because he had graduated on the same day. I suddenly realised who I was talking to as my memory stirred. I asked him if he remembered what he did after the ceremony was over and he recalled that he had gone to the grave of Spurgeon with three other men to leave some flowers on that great preacher's tomb. I asked him if he remembered who the fourth person had been and he thought about that for a while. At last he said, "It was a man from Ireland, he took us in his car." I said, "My dear brother Anatoly, you are looking at that man!" He was really astonished to see me and asked me to wait for a few moments while he dashed inside the building.

In a short time he emerged with another man who walked with a pronounced limp. It was Nicolai another of the students! A short time later Sergei arrived and we had a great reunion. The four of us were together again for the first time in very many years. It seemed a strange coincidence that had united us for the Russian brethren seldom ever meet each other. We had to pose outside Moscow Baptist Church for a photograph which appeared in the Baptist magazine. They ran a feature article about the four of us on a before and after basis.   The Russian brethren all wanted to know why my hair had not turned white yet! Anatoly became the Pastor of the Baptist church in Klin and we have since been able to do a lot of work together there for the Lord. Sergei invited me to come to Leningrad to see the building he had been given.   I was really interested to see it so I took the overnight train to Leningrad.

I had been told the building was in bad shape but nothing prepared me for what I saw on my arrival. It had once been a Russian Orthodox cathedral but it was now a mouldering ruin. Long gone were the seven onion shaped domes, the interior was full of rubbish and the birds were roosting in the rafters. Daylight filtered in through the broken roof and literally nothing remained to indicate that this had ever been a church except the outer shell. It had been closed after the Revolution and then turned into a factory for manufacturing wire ropes and cables. Later on it was used as a paper pulping plant, and in more recent years it had lain derelict. The municipality had given the building to the Christians on the understanding that it would be restored to its former glory. Some people thought Sergei needed to see a psychiatrist when he took up the challenge of restoring this building. We had some discussions together about how I could help with the restoration and at the same time reach out to the needy poor of the city, while also doing something to bring help to the Jews. Wheels were set in motion to try and get permission to bring a lorry full of humanitarian aid to Leningrad, but in the Soviet Union the bureaucratic wheels turned very slowly. When I got back to Northern Ireland I began to plan for my next trip to Russia. There were times when I nearly gave up all thoughts of sending them help as there were so many difficulties to overcome, but ever so slowly things started to change. When at last the permission did come through it seemed to be all in a rush. The Lord was at work making preparations even before we knew it.

CHAPTER TEN

To Russia with Love

One Sunday morning I was preaching at Abbots Cross Congregational Church in Newtownabbey not far from Belfast. We had a very blessed time with the Lord that morning and I came home encouraged from the service. Just as I was entering my house that lunchtime the telephone started to ring. I lifted the receiver and a voice said, "I was at church this morning and the Lord spoke to me." I naturally assumed that the caller was ringing as a result of our morning meeting and I asked if he had been at Abbots Cross. The caller was confused and said, "What do you mean, I was at church in Coleraine." Now it was my turn to be puzzled as I could not understand why he was calling me. "I was at church in Coleraine and the Lord spoke to me and told me that I am to give you my van." he said. I was all the more puzzled and told the man that I did not need a van, there must be some mistake or misunderstanding. The man absolutely insisted that the Lord had instructed him to give me his van. I repeated that I did not need a van and that I had no work for a van, it must be a mistake. Still he insisted that the Lord had spoken to him concerning giving me his van. As he spoke with such conviction I began to wonder if it really was the Lord arranging something. I asked him what kind of a van he was speaking about and he told me it was a Fiat Ducato that could carry about two tonnes. I asked if he would like to lend it to us for a few weeks if something did materialise concerning Russia. He was very definite in his reply, "The Lord said I was to give it to you." I did not even have time to go to look at the van so I sent two other men to check and they came back with a good report like Joshua and Caleb. A few days later the van arrived at my home and no sooner had it come than we began to have lots of work for it to do. Over the next months that van carried tens of thousands of pounds worth of foodstuffs to Loanends and its worth to the work could not be overestimated. Later when it became too old for the work it was used as a trade in for a Mercedes van which we still use regularly. Mervyn had heard the Lord speaking to him about a need we had and he moved to meet it before I was even aware that the need existed! He was really a 'raven' who the Lord sent ahead to provide us with the means to transport lots of the goods He was going to give us from so many different places.

A few weeks later I was in the small country town of Stradbally in the Irish Republic where I was speaking at some meetings for the Faith Mission. I was a guest in the home of David and Betty Stevenson when one day the telephone rang and David said that there was a message for me. I went to the phone and my wife spoke to me rather excitedly.

"Ronnie, permission has come through for you to take a lorry into Russia and I have enquired about a ship and there is space for you in twelve days time. If you do not take the space they do not know when there will next be room. What am I to do?" Pat spoke without pausing for breath as she poured out her story.

I hesitated for only a few moments before I said, "Pat, lets take the space in faith and see what the Lord will do." So we took space on that Finncarriers ship for a lorry we did not have, carrying food we did not have! I was told by a friend that it would take about sixty thousand tins of food to fill a forty foot trailer to capacity. I never did check to see if his estimate was really correct but I realised that it would take a vast amount of material to fill a huge trailer. Two days later I was back home and facing the challenge. Could the Lord send us in the space of ten days all that was needed to fill a lorry? Could he supply us with a lorry and driver and the means to transport it all to Russia?

I was determined that if we were going to do this work it would be entirely a work of faith. We would not make any appeals for money;

neither would we engage in any kind of secular fund raising activity. If the work was of the Lord then He would supply all that was necessary and if He did not then we would know that it was not His will for us to be doing it. I determined that the first day on which I had to put out a begging appeal would be the last day I would ever be engaged in this ministry. We would put God to the test and prove that He could still answer prayer. We would find out if God's 'ravens' really could still fly!

I realised that we could not turn our home into a warehouse again and I was wondering how best to proceed. That same night I was driving home along the Seven Mile Straight returning from a meeting as I had done so often before and as I neared the end of my journey I passed the Loanends Orange Hall. The large hall was in darkness as usual and it seemed that the Lord said to me, "Here is a suitable place for your store, it is seldom used and it is near to your home, ask if you can have the use of it." The next morning I made some enquiries and within an hour I had been given the keys of the hall. I decided to go and inspect the premises for I had never been inside that hall in my life. I would need to get tables organised on which to set things prior to sorting and packing.

I picked up six tins of baked beans as I left my home and then for some reason I drove along the small country Ballymather Road rather than the main Seven Mile Straight which would have been a more direct route. As I drove along the winding road I saw a tractor parked at the road side and as I approached a man came out of the hedgerow.

I knew him to be a neighbour called John Patterson, the father of five girls and a member of the local Prayer Union. I slowed the car and spoke to him out of the window. "Hello John, are you busy today?" I called. John replied that he had just finished planting fifteen thousand trees on his farm as part of an ecological conservation scheme and now he was free. I asked him if he would come with me to Loanends hall to help me set up some tables and he promptly jumped into my car. At the hall we had some difficulty getting the door opened for the lock was stiff but eventually we managed to enter the large musty hall. We found some tables and arranged them in what we thought would be a suitable way and then I asked John to join me in prayer. I placed those six tins of baked beans on one of the tables and we began to pray, I remember that I quoted from Psalm forty five and asked the Lord to open His hand of blessing on our efforts.

When we had finished I said to John, "Those are the first of sixty thousand tins the Lord is going to send us in the next ten days." With his typical Ballymena accent John replied, "I hope you hae the faith to believe it for I hae not." John has proved to be a tower of strength in all the work and I often say that there is a Scripture which has been proved true for me in a special way, "There was a man sent from God whose name was John." ,If ever those words deserved to be applied to another human being besides John the Baptist then that man is certainly John Patterson. Thousands have been blessed through John's faithfulness and many will be in the Glory land as a result of his work. John has put together every one of the thousands of cartons which we have filled with food and clothes. I call him Ballymather's champion Boxer.

In an amazing way the word spread about our project to send the lorry to Russia and the Lord's 'ravens' began to arrive to the hall at Loanends bearing their gifts of food. In a matter of days the hall was filled with all kinds of foodstuffs. The place began to look like a supermarket as the piles of tins grew on the tables by the hour. It was impossible for me to know how it all got there.

I tried to thank as many people as possible personally but it was truly difficult to keep track. Pat did sterling work in our office writing to people and trying to send receipts to all but we would have needed a full time staff to cope properly.

As the thousands of tins gathered at Loanends I became aware of a new problem. The floor was made of wood and was never designed to carry such a load. We tried to spread the weight around as much as possible but I could still hear the timbers creaking. For security reasons I stayed overnight in the hall and during the darkness the sound of the creaking boards more than once had me on the alert.

As the food continued to come in it became clear to us that one lorry would not be enough to carry all the food that the Lord was sending us so we began to make arrangements for a second one. There were many extra difficulties to overcome, both lorries would have to be shipped together, we would need another invitation from Russia and another visa, the transport expenses would be doubled.   Insurance would be needed and of course a suitable driver. The Lord helped us to overcome all these problems and many more while at the same time we continued to be very busy packing the tinned food into boxes.

In order to satisfy the Russian customs we had to fill out a special leaflet and stick it to each box. All the details of the contents had to be noted exactly on each box and then a master copy of the whole had to be supplied to our customs agent.

We borrowed shopping trolleys from a supermarket chain and our helpers walked around the hall and filled the trolleys as they went. They then transferred all the contents of their trolley into the 'family' boxes. At times the hall resembled a factory when the Lord sent us many of His 'ravens' to work there filling up the boxes. At other times the helpers were few and far between, some came for a while and then grew tired of the work and disappeared but the Lord always sent others to fill the gaps.

Throughout all of the work I have never asked any other person besides John Patterson to come to help. Everyone else has come just as they have felt prompted of the Lord. They came not to work for me but to work for Him. Every one of them a 'raven' sent by the Lord to help bear the gifts of food to supply those in such great need in far off Russia. They laboured faithfully not only to send food and aid but to present our Christian testimony in a practical way.

Eventually all the boxes were filled, the lorries were loaded and the drivers were ready to set off. The lorries left from Loanends late at night but it might as well as have been broad daylight for the road was crowded with people who came to see them off.

I remained at home to tidy up the hall and replace the fence. Afterwards I flew out to Helsinki to join the men for the border crossing four days later. I expected that I would return the keys of the hall to its owners and we would be finished with using it. How very wrong I was about this would only be revealed later on, five years have now passed and we still have the keys!

Frank Bell and his friend Mike went again as drivers for us and they had a quiet few days on the ship to Finland. I arrived just in time to meet the lorries coming off the ship and then we drove on our way to the frontier. The severe cold had frozen cascades of water into curious shapes that made interesting viewing as we drove along the road towards the border. When we were about two or three miles from the frontier we stopped to spend some minutes in prayer and then I ran to the phone to call home and ask for more prayer. Pat called around to many of our friends and a chain of prayer was ascending to the Lord as we approached the barriers. The Finnish guards were helpful and nice to us and we passed their formalities without difficulty. Only a few yards now separated us from the Soviet Union and we could see their red flag with it's hammer and sickle insignia fluttering in the cold wind. We passed the first barrier and then the second and eventually came to the main checkpoint. The customs were located in a dilapidated wooden hut that looked from the outside like an old garden shed. Inside things were no better as the wallpaper was ancient and every strip, it seemed, had been taken from a differently patterned roll.

As we presented our customs papers the guard pushed his hat back on his head and said, "Problem." I have since come to the conclusion that the word problem is the most overworked word in the former Soviet Union!

In spite of the problem our papers were eventually stamped by the customs and we were asked, "How many plombs?" The plomb is a wire and lead seal that the customs apply to the trailer door to ensure that it is impossible to open the lorry until final clearance at the destination. The customs officers made sure that the trailer doors were sealed and we prepared to drive on our way when suddenly we had some anxious moments. The driver of our second lorry could not find his keys! Panic set in as he searched in vain through all his pockets. I was eager to be on my way and to finally pass the Russian border.

This particular border held many unpleasant memories for me and it was about the last place where I wanted to linger. It was here that the late Gordon Peters and I had been arrested and detained in 1974. It was here at Torfyanofka that I had last seen my metallic green Peugeot 304S motor car driving away down the road and vanishing from my sight forever. It was here that I had been stripped, beaten, kicked and abused before being deported out of Russia. All for the terrible crime of having one hundred copies of the Bible in my car. Now in the lorry we had many hundreds of Bibles, thousands of Gospels and multitudes of tracts.

It was not a place where I wanted to be any longer than necessary. Our driver decided that he must have set the keys down in the back of the trailer during the check and that they were now sealed inside! There was nothing else for it but to return to the Russian customs and ask them to open the lorry so we could look for the keys. Out came the guards once again and broke off the seals and just at that moment our forgetful driver discovered that he had his keys in the cab all the time! Needless to say the Russians were not too amused and neither was I. Eventually the lorry was sealed up again and we were able to proceed. The roads were snow covered and this helped to fill up the pot holes but it was still like driving on corrugated iron. We passed into the town of Vyborg and wondered if the bridge over the river was going to carry us safely it looked so rickety. The town streets were like something resembling a tank assault course they were so rough.

After about five hours of driving through the forest we entered the city of Leningrad and passed thousands of high rise apartment blocks. At last we reached the church and what rejoicing there was at our coming. In the make shift kitchen Olga was preparing soup and we were glad when it was ready.

As soon as we managed to get our final customs clearance we started to unload the lorries. Many people came to help us as the word spread that we had arrived. The lorries were backed up to the church steps but there was still a long way to carry the heavy boxes up another two flights of stairs. The Russian grandmothers worked like slaves carrying boxes on their shoulders. Heavy tea chests full of tracts were carried as if they were featherweights. Olga was not only good at making soup she could carry boxes better than any man!

I realised now that we had made one mistake when we were packing our boxes. In our desire to be generous we had filled large egg cartons with tins of food and as a result the boxes were too heavy for the old people to carry home. It had not registered with us that most of the people did not have access to a car. They had to take their box home on the tram or the trolley bus and sometimes on the underground. I made a mental note to make sure that we packed smaller boxes if we ever did this again. After unloading most of the boxes at the church we drove to the synagogue where we delivered five hundred Bibles and many boxes of food for the Jewish community. They were not so interested in receiving the New Testament but were glad to take the whole Bible in order to have the Old Testament.

While we were in Leningrad I was invited to go to the office of the Mayor where I had a private meeting with the deputy Mayor of the city. Mr. Sherebekov warmly welcomed me and told me that he was happy we had come to bring aid to the city in this very needy time. He expressed the hope that I would come back soon and indicated that every door was open for us.

I remember him saying, "We made a great mistake in our country about God and the time has now come to rehabilitate our people in their faith. The municipality will extend to you every facility to help you with your work."

CHAPTER ELEVEN

Time for Rest?

When I arrived back after this journey Pat said that she thought I should be ready for a good long rest after all my exertions. How could I rest when the doors of Russia were at last opening! I opened the hall at Loanends again the first Monday morning I was home and within three weeks we had filled another two lorries and were on our way back to Leningrad. As we entered the city this time and drove along the banks of the famous river Neva we passed the Leningrad hotel and I pointed out to Frank that this was where I used to stay when I came to the city during the time of Brezhnev. As we talked together I mentioned that there had been a horrific fire at the hotel the previous winter which had claimed twenty nine lives. The fire service had been inadequately equipped and could do little to rescue the people. It was during this conversation that we had the idea of trying to present the city with one of our fire appliances as a kind of token gesture. We made it a matter of prayer and asked the Lord to provide a fire appliance and an ambulance for the city.

The work of restoration at the church was going on slowly so I organised a team of twenty five men to travel out to assist with the rebuilding. Those men made a big contribution to the building work although they found difficulty at times in coping with the circumstances. The team stayed for a month and then travelled home while I stayed on for another two months to continue with work on the building and to assist with the ministry. This was a very valuable time and I learned a lot more about Russian life. A few weeks before I was due to come home the Communists attempted a coup against the government. It was a very tense and dangerous time with lots of demonstrations on the streets. The tanks were reported to be approaching Leningrad but were halted some miles away. Barricades were built across the city streets in preparation for civil war. I was present at the huge rally at the palace square when it was declared that the Communist Party was outlawed. I was standing right at the Maryinsky Palace when the red flag was lowered. Those were very historic days as Boris Nicolaevitch Yeltsin began to stamp his influence on Russia. The Soviet Union disintegrated into chaos and the process of reform gathered pace. I was not concerned with the politics of it all but only with the fact that here was an unprecedented opportunity for people in Russia to hear about the love of Jesus.

I returned home intending to spend a few weeks in Northern Ireland speaking at meetings and encouraging supporters. Our plan was that we would fill another lorry with food and travel out with that one lorry, the ambulance and the fire appliance.

Instead of a happy homecoming I arrived back to hear devastating news. The house had been broken into and all my office equipment had been stolen including two computers and all of our records. Much of the text of this book on which I had previously been working was on the hard disk of one computer and was entirely lost! Then the fire appliance was not nearly ready as the people who were responsible for converting it to left hand drive were dragging their feet. I was disappointed especially at the loss of my writing and of all our records. The devil told me we would never be able to fill another lorry now for we would not be able to notify people about our plans. No one would know that we needed prayer. I was feeling down but then the Lord reminded me that He does not depend on our sending out prayer letters to meet the needs, His 'ravens' still fly.

We turned to the Lord in prayer again and He demonstrated His power wonderfully by way of answer. We filled not just one lorry but a convoy of several all loaded with love. It was wonderful to have all these lorries going, it was wonderful to have ten tonnes of frozen meat, it was wonderful to have the ambulance, the fire appliance and all the rest but I was delighted most of all that my dear friend Gordon Peters was coming with us. Gordon had not been back to Russia since our arrest and deportation in 1974 and now he decided to come with us. It was November and we were very busy loading all the lorries, the work was hard, difficult and tiring. Usually I worked every day at the hall until about seven in the evening and then dashed off to speak at a church somewhere. I was just getting ready to leave one evening when a man called at the door while I was still in the process of putting on my shirt. He was a stranger to me but he gave me an envelope containing a fuel card and a map of the stations where we could fill all the lorries with diesel on our route at his expense. Joe Baird of Joe Baird Haulage was a 'raven' sent by the Lord to help our convoy on its way. Then the phone rang and this time it was a friend from the Island of Arran calling to ask about what we were doing at that moment. This friend of ours works for P & O Ferries, when I told him about the convoy he said that when we were ready to leave we should just go to the booking office in Larne and mention the name of The Eschol Trust.

With these few delays I was by now running late so I dashed to the car to get away to my meeting. As I roared out the gate I saw my Mother and Dad coming out of their house to go to the Prayer Union. Ever since Dad trusted the Lord he went every week to the Prayer Union and participated in public prayer.

I remember saying to the Lord that night as I drove away that I was so happy to see my Dad going to the prayer meeting rather than to a Public house. I came back later that night and went straight to Loanends to carry on with the work, John Patterson was waiting for me at the hall door. "You better go up to Rea's house" John said to me as I arrived. Willie Rea's was where the Prayer Union was held. I was puzzled as to why I should go there and then John said to me through his tears, "Your Father has passed away tonight." I rushed to the house and there were all the members of the prayer union sitting in a circle just as they had been during the prayer time.

My Dad was lying on the floor with his Bible open on his chest. Mother was sitting looking sad but calm. Dad had been praying to the Lord and just as he came to the end of his prayer without any noise or any sign of pain he gave a sigh and went to Heaven. What a wonderful way to pass from this world. To very few is such a privilege given, to pass from the prayer meeting directly into the presence of the Master! To be actually in the very act of speaking to the Lord at the moment of hearing His homecall.

I was very sad and yet I felt it would be a sin to grieve too much for the Lord had kept all His promises before he took my Dad to be with Himself. My sadness was mixed with joy at the sure knowledge that Dad had gone to be with Christ which is far better. Work at the hall was suspended for two days until after the funeral but I knew that he would not have wanted me to change all our plans to help the needy just because he was gone from us. We had talked with the fire men about the possibility of having a praise service but it did not seem to be the right time for such a service of praise so I did not proceed with that.

In spite of the sadness of the sudden bereavement I went through with the rest of the project. On the day of our departure Ulster Television came to the harbour at Larne to do an interview with me. I never seek for publicity on the media, we are too busy doing the work to spend much time going to do interviews to talk about it!

While I was detained with U.T.V. Pat went into the office of P & O at Larne to collect the tickets for shipping all the vehicles across to Cairnryan. When she came out she asked me, "How much do you think we had to pay for this crossing?" I was expecting it to be several thousand pounds for all our vehicles. The cost was just under fifty pounds for the harbour dues! The lorries were shipped over at no cost to us. My friend from Arran had proved to really be a 'raven' sent by the Lord at just the right time. We did not seek him out, we did not tell him we were going to Russia. He just felt led of the Lord to telephone from Arrran to ask what we were doing and when he found out what was happening the Lord used him to send blessing to thousands of people. It is such a thrill to see the Lord provide without any human manipulation being involved.

We had a good trip out to Russia, the Baltic Sea was kind to us and not too rough. We drove across Finland through the snow and came to Leningrad. There was a big open air civic ceremony for the handing over of the equipment we had brought and afterwards we proclaimed the Gospel. At the end of the open air meeting we distributed tracts to the large crowd. Gordon Peters went into the midst of the throng and was mobbed by people wanting to take the literature from him. When it was all gone Gordon turned and called to me saying, "I need more, I need more." A little man who had no legs came along the street on a kind of skate board and Gordon ran to him. He gave Gordon his name and address and Gordon brought it to me saying, "Ronnie we have to help that poor creature, how can he manage to line up for food." That afternoon I put Gordon into a taxi with lots of boxes of food and he delivered it to that needy man. Sadly not many months after that trip Gordon too was suddenly called home to be with the Lord. He was just forty seven years of age and seemed to have many good years before him. I miss very much his unique personality and his friendship. We came through a lot together in Russia in 1974. I just rejoice that he was able to go back with me once more before the Lord took him home. It was so special for me to have him along. It is good to have the assurance that one day we will meet again.

CHAPTER TWELVE

Hospital 26

I was first introduced to Hospital 26 in rather a strange way. I was standing at the reception desk in the Moscow hotel waiting to make a telephone call when the man next to me emitted a loud sigh. By way of starting a conversation I said to him, "It can't be as bad as that surely." His reply was not what I expected. "It is far worse than that. Three days ago my wife was mugged at Petrodvorets and her thigh is broken. Our party has gone on to Kazakstan with the guide and I am left alone here and I don't know what to do." When I realised the man's terrible plight I quickly brought the Russian pastor who was waiting outside for me into the hotel and we got on the telephone to try to organise some help.

Then the three of us went to the hospital to visit the poor woman. I found her in a single room where the light did not work, lying in an unmade bed in considerable distress. We got the light repaired and summoned the doctor and soon had things arranged for an air ambulance to fly the woman to Holland for treatment before returning her to her home in New Zealand. I had the joy of praying with her and she shed many tears of gratitude. The lady was a patient in Hospital 26. That introduction led to a contact with the hospital and now we were presenting the ambulance and many beds to the hospital.

After the official handing over of the equipment we had a luncheon with the Mayor and several of the leading dignitaries. Next to me sat the chief administrator of Hospital 26, a lady doctor called Helen. In the course of our lunch time conversation she asked me what I could tell her about our hospitals in Northern Ireland. I began to give her my opinion concerning the wonderful work done at our Royal Victoria Hospital and spoke about Dr. Pantridge and the flying cardiac ambulance service. Then I began to speak about the Belfast City Hospital and the way they are famous for renal treatment. Helen was impressed by the talk and said, "Oh how I wish we could treat all our kidney patients." As I asked her to enlarge on what she was meaning I became aware that because of a shortage of dialysis equipment kidney patients were dying prematurely. I said, "That is awful, we must do something about it. What will you say if I tell you that I will go home and pray and ask the Lord to give me a kidney machine for your hospital." Helen asked me if I was a millionaire who could afford to buy such expensive equipment.

I made it clear to her that I was certainly not a millionaire and never would be but that I knew the Lord was able to supply because He owns the cattle on a thousand hills. Helen looked at me and said, "You know I am an atheist I was brought up to believe that there is no God. But today I have seen all the things you have brought here and I know that if you say the Lord can do it then I am sure that He could do it." We began to pray earnestly for the Lord to supply a kidney machine and the Lord began to move by His spirit to arrange things.

John Neil was a good friend of mine for many years, he sang with the Abbots Cross choir and in spite of the fact that he was blind John lived life to the full. John before his conversion was interested in the world of clubs and drinking but then he was laid low with kidney disease. In reality he should have been dead many times over but the Lord spared him. He went through a kidney transplant and survived longer than almost anyone else in Europe. In a wonderful way John found a friend in the Lord Jesus Christ and trusted Him for the Salvation of his soul. I enlisted John's help for our kidney dialysis project as he knew all the right people. Together we went to the Belfast City Hospital and arranged an interview with Dr. James Douglas the consultant nephrologist. John introduced me to Dr. Douglas and it was not long before we were deep into conversation about kidneys and the Lord. This wonderful doctor gave me every encouragement to push on with the project and pulled out all the stops to help me get a dialysis machine. I wanted to present the hospital in Leningrad with a brand new machine and when I asked Dr. Douglas to order it for me he hesitated. "Have the people been so generous, do you have all the money to pay for it?" the good doctor asked. I think he was a little worried in case he would be left in the lurch with a bill for more that twenty thousand pounds. I think he might have been even more worried if he had known that we were walking absolutely by faith and that I did not have even one single pound towards it that day! I said to Dr. Douglas, "There is no point in two of us worrying about the same thing, so I will worry about the money and you just take care about placing the order for me." I went off to Israel a few days later for the feast of the Passover and when I came back after two weeks I called Dr. Douglas to see if there was any progress. Nothing had happened in my absence so I decided to put through a call to the manager of the company which sold the dialysis equipment. If Mr. Chris Seymour was surprised by my call he did not show it. I told him I wanted the kidney machine put on a lorry and sent to me right away that very morning.

I promised that as soon as I would receive the invoice he would have our cheque for the payment by return. How good the Lord was in answering prayer, the machine arrived and before the invoice came to hand the Lord sent His 'ravens' with all the money that was needed to pay for it and to transport it to Russia. Dr. Douglas arranged for a team to come out from Belfast City Hospital to install the machine and to show the Russians how to treat the first patients. Vanita, Mary and Derek volunteered to come to help me and were a great team to have along. B.C.H paid them as if they were working at home and even found the money to pay for their flight tickets. They did a great job and many people are alive today who would have already been dead but for the treatment they have been able to receive on that machine. Every patient in the dialysis unit of that hospital is lying on a bed from Northern Ireland, and a lot of other equipment has been given to the hospital to help them. Many times we have had the privilege of preaching the Gospel in Hospital 26 and I have had the joy of seeing many of the kidney patients placing their trust in the Lord Jesus Christ. We continue to supply equipment as the Lord provides and every time I go to St. Petersburg (as the city is now called) I make sure to bring boxes of food for the kidney patients.

John Neill has now gone to be with the Lord and for him it is far better for his eyes are open and he has seen the face of Jesus. Without John Neill I might never have managed to put the kidney machine in Hospital 26. I will never forget John for his gracious spirit and his willingness to help others with similar problems to his own. John wanted them to live a little longer so that they could hear the story of a Saviour's love and give their lives to Him.

Many months after installing the machine at the hospital, my telephone rang one day at home in Northern Ireland. To my surprise it was a call from the United States of America. I was curious to find it was a call from Seattle from the North West Kidney Centre. A doctor from there had been in St. Petersburg and he had visited the hospital and now he was calling me. Was there some emergency? Had the machine broken down? Dr. Chris Blagg had expressed surprise when he saw the new kidney machine during his visit and the young Russian kidney specialist Dr. Boris Nicolaivitch explained how I had given it to the hospital. Dr. Blagg was calling me with a rather interesting proposition. The North West Kidney Centre was prepared to give me another kidney machine free of charge. There was only one snag in the whole proposition, the machine was in Seattle in Dr. Blagg's office and it was up to me to find out how to get it from the USA to Russia. It was quite a challenge to my faith, could the Lord find a way to get that machine to me? I began to pray about it very seriously during the next weeks and I also called several airlines to try to get someone to fly it over for me. Delta, United, American and British Airways were only some of those I tried. The price for air cargo was prohibitive for it was quite a heavy machine. Did the Lord have a 'raven' somewhere waiting to bring that kidney machine over?

I had organised a youth camp in the Republic of Belarus and our plan was to take a bus with fifty four of our young people. In order to help the young people to enjoy the camp I was driving out in our lorry at the same time with a large consignment of food and Christian literature. On our arrival at the border between Germany and Poland there was a long delay in the channel for lorries. The bus with the young people was able to continue but I had to wait in the line all through the night. Just as the day was breaking I was cleared to pass the border and drove on into Poland. As I was driving along I was praying to the Lord about different things that were on my heart and one of those things was the kidney machine that was standing in Seattle. Suddenly the Lord reminded me of someone I had met back in April and impressed on me that I should contact this person at once.

I had been travelling home to Northern Ireland from Israel on a British Airways flight after enjoying leading a group for the Passover celebrations. My friends were all resting and I decided to take a walk around the aeroplane. In the galley at the rear several members of the crew were having their coffee break and enjoying some strawberries and as I passed by one of them offered some to me.

In a few moments I was in the galley along with the crew members and as we ate the strawberries I spoke to the flight crew about the Lord. As we talked together several things were mentioned and I began to tell them about our work in Russia. Later when I had returned to my seat one of the men from the crew came to me and presented me with his visiting card saying that maybe we would meet again some day. I put the card into my pocket and when I arrived home I put it on the shelf in my office along with dozens of other such cards where it was promptly forgotten.

As I drove along the road in the direction of Warsaw that morning the Lord really impressed on me that we should call this person. I stopped at the small farm where I had arranged to meet up with the young people in the event of our being separated at the border. I asked the elderly lady there if I could use her telephone. After some initial difficulties I managed to get through to Pat. It was still very early in the morning in Northern Ireland and it was a sleepy voice that answered the telephone. I explained where the card was in the office and asked Pat to call Ed Jarrett for me to tell him about the kidney machine and see what would happen. At first she was very reluctant to make the call saying that probably he would not remember me and that she would not know what to say to him. After some long distance persuasion Pat made the call and the Lord began to move again in answer to our prayers. Just a few days later Ed was transferred from the flights to Israel to the flight to Seattle! On arrival after his first flight Ed made contact with Dr. Blagg by telephone and then went to the Kidney centre and checked out the machine for weight and size.

On his own initiative he approached several BA staff members who donated their own cargo concessions for the next twelve months and between them they brought the machine over on the next flight. When Ed telephoned to tell me, I was overjoyed at the prospect of getting the machine brought in to London Heathrow, I was ready to drive there in our van to collect it. Ed said that he thought that would be too much trouble for me and actually had the machine flown directly into Belfast! That kidney machine flew all the way from Seattle to Belfast without me having to pay one penny either for the purchase of it or for the transport. Without a doubt God's 'ravens' do still fly, Dr. Chris Blagg was one of them. Ed Jarrett and Jackie Magnus of the BA 747 fleet were real flying 'ravens' who the Lord used to help us do His work.

Now that the machine was in Northern Ireland we had to solve another problem concerning it. As it had come from America it was set up to run on 110v electricity so we would need to convert it to 220v. An initial enquiry in Northern Ireland seemed to indicate that it would be very costly to do this so I decided to telephone the manufacturers in the United States. The lady I spoke to was interested in what we were doing and proved to be very helpful indeed. That lady made sure that all the technical information was faxed to me with the circuit diagrams. In the course of our transatlantic telephone call she mentioned that her company had an expert in England and that she would contact him with a request for help.

It was only a short time later that I received a call from Andy Mossan in Leicester. As Andy and I spoke about the machine he told me that he was going to be in Belfast at the Royal Victoria Hospital installing some new scanning equipment the very next day. We arranged that Andy would come to see our machine and then we would decide what to do. The next morning Aldergrove airport was closed due to dense fog and Andy did not manage to get to Belfast that day. I was a bit disappointed as I had been looking forward to getting things underway. I should not have worried for the Lord as usual was at work all the time. A few days later Andy called to say he was at the Royal Victoria Hospital and that he would call me as soon as he was free. He had used the interval to collect all the parts needed to convert the machine and was ready to do the work that very day. It was about three pm. in the afternoon when he called to say he was free if I could come to collect him. Andy said he would wait for me on the main drive through the hospital somewhere.

I was so delighted at the prospect that I forgot to ask him what he looked like. It was only as I was driving to the hospital that I suddenly asked myself how I was going to recognise this stranger. I should not have worried about it, when I drove along the main road through the hospital there was a very distinctive looking person standing with a brief-case in his hand. As I pulled over to ask if it was Andy he jumped into my car and said, "You must be Ronnie McCracken." Time was short as Andy had to catch the evening plane to England so it was straight to work in the entrance hall of our house. As he worked away Andy asked me to tell about the machine and why we had it in our house. I told him about the things the Lord had been doing and he was impressed. "I am not religious at all but if I was going to be then this is the kind of religion I would believe in," He said.

When I asked Andy for his bill for doing the work he refused to accept any payment saying that it was his donation to the cause. Andy did not even have time for a cup of coffee as every moment was pre-cious but he finished all the work on the machine before we dashed to the airport. On the way he asked me if I would like another kidney dialysis machine for the hospital in St. Petersburg! Three days later Andy called to say that he had shipped not one but two more kidney machines to me. They were absolutely free of charge and he paid the bill for the road transport to get them to me. A week later when our next lorry set off for Russia it was carrying not one but three more kidney machines for Hospital 26.

It has been really remarkable how the Lord has provided, it has been remarkable how the Lord so often has sent His 'ravens' in the most unexpected ways. Never once have I made an appeal for money to carry on the work. Never once have we sent out a letter pleading with people for donations. We have of course sought to inform our friends about what we are doing and we have made many appeals for prayer for the work. The Lord has been so faithful in providing all the means to carry on this work.

CHAPTER THIRTEEN

Chernobyl Children

During all these many trips to the former Soviet Union I had heard a lot of people speaking about the Chernobyl catastrophe. We had sent several lorries to the Ukraine which had suffered a great deal from the fall out. Professor Abraham Mintz is a Jewish friend who assisted us greatly with our work there in Kiev. Dr. Joseph Entis and his wife Mina opened their home to Pastor Joel and I because we had helped their son Sergei and his family in Italy when they were on the way to America. From these dear friends and others I had heard a lot about the effects of Chernobyl on the children and I began to make it a matter of prayer. I was asking the Lord what He would have us to do concerning the children. Many years ago when we were conducting missions in different areas of Ireland we always had special meetings for the children. I really loved working with children in these meetings and it was an area of the ministry which I really missed very much.

After about two years of thinking and praying about this I received an invitation to meet with a group of children from Belarus who were in England. I flew to Liverpool to meet the group and after some discussion with the leaders I agreed to try to organise the first ever group of Chernobyl Children to come to Northern Ireland. We would see how the Lord would lead concerning the matter.

One morning a few days later I was sitting in the office typing letters when Pat came in and looked over my shoulder to see what I was doing. Then she said to me, "Ronnie do you know that it is going to be our wedding anniversary in July?" I replied that of course I knew it was coming up again but she went on to ask me if I knew which one it was. I had to think for a bit about that for I would have been in big trouble if I said the wrong number! Eventually I recalled that it was going to be twenty five years since our wedding day. A quarter of a century! I stopped my typing and we discussed for a few minutes what we could do to mark such a milestone. We could go to visit some of our workers in South Africa, that would be really great. Or we could go on a long promised trip to Asia to see our Chinese young people. Many of the young people who have studied in Ireland have invited us to go to visit them in Hong Kong, Malaysia and Singapore but I have never been able to find the time to go. That would be nice, we could see all their families. As we contemplated all the possibilities I turned to Pat and said, "There is really only one thing I would like to do, I would like to bring twenty five of those children from Chernobyl for a break in Northern Ireland. Instead of us going off to have a good time lets do something for these needy children." Immediately Pat agreed with me and said, "Yes lets do that."

Once again we set the wheels in motion for another big project. I went to Minsk in Belarus and made all the arrangements for the children's travel to Northern Ireland. We planned to bus them to Warsaw and then fly them by British Airways to London and on to Belfast. Two teachers from Belarus would accompany the children and act as interpreters. It was my request that half of the children would be Jewish and half Gentiles. When all the arrangements were completed I travelled back home to Northern Ireland and a few days later I received a call. The caller wanted to know if it would be possible for me to take one more child. A boy from Brest called Andrei Liebenbaum was ill and it was thought that the change would be good for him. I immediately agreed to take Andrei as well, the number twenty five was only symbolic.

The children were looking forward to coming to us and we were anxiously praying to the Lord for His provision to bring them. I had all the twenty eight seats reserved with British Airways and from time to time I received a call from their Groups Manager asking how things were progressing. Then one day he called to say that we had just another seven days before we would have to pay for the seats or else lose them. There was a lot of pressure for seats on the flight and I suppose that BA needed to be sure we would not let them down. At that moment we had some of the money but we were still a long way from being able to pay the airline. Once again we were cast on the Lord for His help and support. Several gifts came to hand and two days later I received a telephone call in the morning. The caller said that she was from Northern Telecom and asked if I could come to the factory that morning. I hesitated for a moment but then agreed to go. The lady who was calling asked if I could go to the factory right away. Somewhat puzzled I set out to go to the Northern Telecom factory and on my arrival I was met at the gate by two ladies who were strangers to me. They took me inside and gave me a cup of coffee in the canteen. As we stood there drinking the coffee they said, "Its a very cold morning outside." I agreed but at the same time I was asking myself what I was doing standing there drinking coffee in a factory canteen. One lady began to explain that she had been reading a newspaper article about Chernobyl and it had deeply touched her heart. This kind hearted woman had asked her work mates to give her a donation for Chernobyl children and she had collected a sum of money from them.

After she had it collected she was at a loss as to how to proceed to give it to some worthy cause to help the children. For a while she thought that she might give it to the newspaper where she had read the article. Just as she was thinking about all this someone came into work one day and told her that they had been at a church where they heard some talk about our project. Immediately the lady had contacted me and so that was why I was there in the factory. That woman, a complete stranger, proceeded to hand me a cheque for the money she had collected and I was deeply grateful to her. I looked at the cheque and noticed that it was for four hundred pounds, exactly the amount I still needed to complete the payment to British Airways. I told the ladies that I was astonished that the Lord had used them to meet the need in this way, they had not been to any meetings to hear about the project but the Lord had put his hand on them to bless the children. The ladies were moved to tears as they realised that they had been vital to the project. One of the ladies then asked if it would be possible to see the children when they came, would they be allowed to come to the church to meet them? I declared that everyone who worked in the factory could come to the church to meet the children and that they would all be very welcome. I think that gave the ladies an idea for they then asked me if I would bring the children to visit the factory. They could sing choruses and I could speak to the people there about God. I was only too delighted to arrange it and the day was fixed there and then.

That very same afternoon I went to the office of British Airways in Belfast and spoke with Mr. Colin McCaw the group manager. I paid the bill and received the flight tickets for all the group. Colin even gave me a British Airways flight bag as a present before I left with the tickets. Everything was now in place and we were eagerly awaiting the children's coming. It was wonderful to wait at Aldergrove for the arrival of the children with a reception committee of interested friends. The children were a bit overcome with it all when they saw balloons and welcome posters in Russian. Then they were on to the Ulsterbus and off to Ballycraigy church where the house parents were waiting to take their new children home. I was so happy that the Lord had performed the miracle and brought these children to us. Every morning they came to the church for Bible lessons and every afternoon they travelled by Ulsterbus to different places in Northern Ireland. I will never forget what happened when we took them the first Monday afternoon to Whitehead. One little girl looked at Belfast Lough and said, "Ooh is that really the sea." Belarus is a landlocked republic and many children have never had the chance to breathe the sea air. That day as we walked along the promenade I was praising the Lord from the depths of my soul.

I was saying to myself as I walked along, "The children are really here. It is not just a dream. The Lord has really answered prayer and here they are walking where I used to walk when I was a boy." Then as I looked at them I noticed something very important, most of their footwear was in appalling condition. One boy had only a pair of bedroom slippers on his feet! When I arrived home later that night I said to Pat, "Did you see the youngsters feet? They have not a pair of shoes between them. We will have to do something at once." Do something we did. Next day we drove to Sandy Row in Belfast to the well known Reid's shoe shop. The sales girl was surprised when I asked for twenty six pairs of trainers. There was a big commotion in the shop and nearly all the shoe boxes were down on the floor. Feet were measured and then measured again. Colours were discussed and minds were changed more than once and it was a glorious confusion. When all was finished the children stood in the shop and sang to the workers and those amazed customers who happened to be in buying shoes. They sang from their little hearts the choruses they had just learned for the first time in their lives. 'Jesus Love is very wonderful' and 'My God is so big, so strong and so mighty, there's nothing that He cannot do.' I think there was not a dry eye in the shop. Here were children who had never known about Jesus love until a few days earlier and now they were so happy to sing about it.

I asked myself what was wrong with our own people who have known about it all their lifetime and yet still reject that love. I think it is time a lot of our people gave their hearts to Jesus in a simple childlike way. Stanley Reid the owner of the shop made sure that we were not charged the full amount of the bill for all the shoes. Later on we repeated the exercise in another shoe shop in East Belfast where we bought all the children good strong winter shoes for going to school. It was a big thrill to be able to do it for the children.

The friends at Northern Telecom were waiting for us to come for lunch at the factory and so to the factory we went. The lunch was terrific, I think the chips were piled up like small mountains and were more than a man could eat. The staff listened as the children sang to them and I spoke to them about the Saviour's love for us all. Out on the factory floor there were telephones set up for the children to experiment with and talk to each other They sang again and again to all the workers in the different departments. At the end as we prepared to leave the ladies were waiting to hug all the children and give them a carrier bag full of good things. I have a sense of humour so I lined up with the children for my hug and bag of goodies. There was none for me but the ladies did have something, they had a cheque for one thousand two hundred and forty five pounds.

The Northern Telecom workers had spontaneously given this money to help with the expenses for the children. I will never forget the kindness and generosity of the Northern Telecom staff and workers. I will always remember the 'ravens' who the Lord sent to us from that factory to bless the children, and I will always be grateful to them. Many others helped us with the children and if I were to write about all then this book would become too large by far. The house parents fell in love with the children and wanted to keep them. The church allowed us to put on a wonderful evening of praise with the children that was unforgettable. Our MP, Clifford Forsyth, summed it up for us all as he was leaving the church that evening when he said, "I cannot remember when anything moved me so much or brought me so close to the Lord."

After two weeks at Ballycraigy we moved to County Fermanagh to Ulster's Lakeland for a wonderful week on Lusty Beg island in Lough Erne. For all those who came to help it was really an unforgettable week. The Bible lessons continued every day and there were all kinds of activities as well. There was boating and fishing and on the last night we had the first ever fireworks display on Lusty Beg.

All too soon it was all over and we found ourselves at the airport saying goodbye. Tears were flowing all round as the children sang their choruses to us for the last time. Even the girl at the counter who was collecting the tickets started to cry and the black stuff she had on her eyes started to run down her face. She looked at me through her tears and said, "This is awful, I don't even know them and I can't stop crying." Just when the children were getting too emotional about it all I told them not to cry because I had a special announcement to make. I was going to load up the lorry and in three weeks time I would come to visit them all. I would come to every house and bring presents for them and their families. The children cheered up at the prospect and in three weeks I was on my way to Belarus to visit them all. The visit of the children to Northern Ireland was a time of very special blessing for us as we saw the Lord provide everything for them. I felt that it would have been a mistake to simply bid the children goodbye at the airport. I wanted to meet all the families and to see the circumstances in which the children lived.

I had been away from home in Norway for a wonderful holiday week with a small group and on my return to England my wife and Wesley Ballantine were waiting to meet me with the lorry on the road near Carlisle. I swapped vehicles with them, they took my car and travelled back to Northern Ireland while I took the lorry and set off for

Harwich to catch the ship to Hamburg. I was driving along quite nicely that night making reasonable time when suddenly something happened to the lorry. There was a loss of power and then behind me I could see in the mirror dense clouds of smoke. I could still drive but no one behind me could see anything. I turned off the main road and after some few minutes I found a place where I could stop. There was nothing else for it but to wait for daylight. That old Volvo lorry was more then ten years old and had no place for sleeping so the night was long. When daylight came I jacked up the cab to check the engine and there I saw the tell tale signs of a blown turbo. There was no doubt about it and I knew that it was not some simple thing that I could fix on the road. I let the cab back down and then I sat there for some time wondering what to do. I decided that I would need to spend some time in prayer speaking to the Lord about it. I was parked on a quiet country road that was like a leafy lane and not much traffic was passing by so there did not seem any chance of some help arriving. As I was sitting there praying I asked the Lord to send me help.

I was not even sure exactly where I was and I certainly did not know where to go to look for assistance. Just at that moment a car drew up alongside me and a woman got out. This lady apparently passed earlier and had come back to ask about the sign on the lorry which declared 'God is Love'. I explained to her all about what we were doing and then told her that I was stranded there because of a breakdown. It was unusual for a woman to stop and approach a lorry on such a lonely road. The lady explained to me that the sign had interested her because she had just recently become a Christian. I then told her how I had been praying for help and she was so excited to think that the Lord had sent her to be His helper for me. In a few moments she left me only to return later with a mechanic. The mechanic had a look and confirmed my fears about the turbo and then used his mobile phone to call a breakdown waggon. As we waited for the waggon to arrive the lady offered to take me to her home for breakfast but I declined her kind offer saying I would need to be there when the breakdown vehicle arrived. Eventually it came and we prepared to tow my lorry to the nearest garage. Just as I was about to go I asked the lady if she would give me her name and address so that I could send her a letter of thanks later on. When the woman said to me, "My name is Liz Wren." I began to laugh and she was puzzled. "Why are you laughing, is my name so funny?" she asked me. I am not sure if she understood my Ulster sense of humour or not but the thought that came to me that morning was, the Lord sent the ravens to Elijah but all He needed to send to me was a Wren! Liz Wren was really a 'raven' sent by the Lord to help me when I was absolutely stranded.

The garage I was towed to was Duffields of East Anglia the main Volvo agents where they soon got the old Volvo sorted out and on the road again. There is not space here to write everything about that visit to the homes of the children in Belarus. The children were so happy to see me in their own homes and everywhere I went I had to eat. I was particularly touched to visit the villages where some of the children lived in quite primitive conditions. Life in Belarus in general is much better than in Russia. The main need really is to share the Gospel message.

Even before a year passed we had another children's group visiting us, this time from the Messianic Congregation in Minsk. Almost all of the children who came with that group were Jewish. Thirty five of us lived at Stricklands Holiday Home in Bangor where we had a fantastic time. This group were all members of the same congregation and they were able to sing as a choir when they visited our churches.

Later on we had yet another group of thirty one children who came to Northern Ireland and lived on the famous Antrim coast. Perhaps our biggest effort was for a group which we took to Israel for the tenth anniversary of the Chernobyl accident. The children were ecstatic to be in the Holy Land and it was so special for me to be with the Jewish children in the land of their ancestors. The Lord provided for all these children without any appeals from us to the public. We made no requests for money in the press or on the media. Our only appeal was to the Lord in the place of prayer. Time and again I reminded myself of the words of Hudson Taylor the founder of China Inland Mission, "You may depend upon it gentlemen, God's work done in God's way will never lack God's supply." Time and again the Lord proved to us that His ravens still fly bringing His supply in time of need.

CHAPTER FOURTEEN

Tin Soldiers for the Lord

A s we continued with the work of helping the needy in Russia I was always concerned about the danger of the food not reaching the people who really need it. There are so many gangsters and mafia people in Russia these days and it is very difficult to escape their clutches. The black market flourishes and lots of humanitarian aid ends up getting sold in kiosks on the street. I did not want to work so hard to bring things to Russia only to see it disappear into the coffers of the mafia. This was something that I was constantly praying about as we sent each consignment. I made it my policy that I had personally to be present each time the lorries arrived, never did we simply send a lorry off to Russia with a driver. As far as possible I went to individuals who I knew well and left food at their homes for distribution to their needy neighbours. I rented a store in St. Petersburg where I maintained a supply of food and clothes which were distributed to the needy by a young lady from Northern Ireland. Roisin McElroy was studying Russian in a language school in St. Petersburg and the store I rented was in the same building. Roisin had access to the store and freedom to distribute whatever she wanted to needy people she came in contact with.

Even with all these safeguards I was still anxious about the food getting to the right people. One night when I had gone home from Loanends to get some rest the Lord gave me an idea. I could make a special label to put on every tin and packet which would tell the people that these were free gifts and explain why they were given. I wondered why I had not thought of it earlier it seemed so simple. In fact it was not just so simple to do it. I needed to find a printer who could print adhesive labels to stick on the tins. The labels needed to be in Russian so I needed to find someone who could translate what I required and then print out a master copy. Where could I find someone who could do such a thing? I was given a contact in England and I called the lady on the telephone. As I introduced myself to her she said, "How very strange, last night we were at a prayer meeting and the speaker mentioned you and the work you have been doing and asked us to pray for you. We were praying for you last night and now today you call me." It was a big surprise for me, I have never preached in that area in my life and I do not know how the speaker got to hear about the work we were doing. I had no idea they were praying for me there. As I explained why I was calling and the idea I had in my mind the lady became more and more interested. "I have a friend from Russia who is studying here and she will translate everything for you and I have a computer which can print in Russian. Fax me what you want and I will do it right away." Within a few minutes I had the text ready to fax to her. It said,

---

FREE GIFT OF FOOD
Because
"God so loved the world that he gave His only begotten son that whosoever believeth on Him should not perish but have everlasting life." John 3:16.
If you want to know more please write to:-
PO BOX 5, Crumlin, N. Ireland.
A gift from Christians in Northern Ireland as a token of friendship and love in the name of God.

In less than an hour I received the master copy of the label through the fax machine and very soon a printer in the small town of Banbridge was engaged to produce tens of thousands of these labels. When we received the first batch we set to work and in the next three days we managed to stick labels on to ninety thousand tins. It all had to be done by hand but the Lord sent in a good team of workers to labour at this important task. Every tin of food literally became a Gospel messenger as well as being protected from being sold on the black market. Many moving letters have come to us as a result of these labels being on the tins. I have been astonished at how the tins have travelled to the most remote places right across the vast land of Russia. Letters have come from as far away as Vladivostock in the far east of the country.

One day I was in a town about fifty miles from Moscow when a friend asked me to go with him to a village where he had some business. After driving for about an hour he asked me, "Ronnie do you think that this car can drive over fields?" I was not sure if it was a joke but I soon realised it was not when we turned off the road into a field which was crossed by a barely discernible track. Even now in October it was difficult to keep the car moving, I wondered what it would be like in winter. Off to our left I could see an almost deserted military base in the forest. The main contingent of soldiers are long gone and the place is falling into disrepair. Then in front of us I began to see some little wooden houses stretching out in a long row. We stopped the car and stepped out into the brisk air to look around. I asked my friend if I should lock the car and he began to laugh at the very idea that it might be necessary. All around us was forest and fields, we entered the house of my friend and looked around. The garden was overgrown and neglected, in the middle stood a rusting water tank which catches the winter rain and snow. There is no water supply in Evjalova so the people use the rain water for washing and have to carry their drinking water from the military base. Next to the water tank stood the privy, a primitive affair raised up on wooden blocks with an air space of about three feet underneath. A rough plank serves the users as a seat while they balance precariously over a malodorous heap below. Certainly in winter no one will linger here for a moment more than necessary because of the cold.

Only about a third of the houses are occupied now and most of them have elderly inhabitants. My friend had come to pay some taxes on a house that belonged to his relatives. He told me that once someone was taken ill and needed to be hospitalised but the ambulance could not reach the village because of the snow, the sick person had to be carried to a main road about a mile away. On another occasion someone died and it was impossible for the lorry bringing the box for the body to get through, the corpse had to be carried out to the lorry. We entered the next house to visit the people who lived there and to leave the money for the taxes. The front door seemed to open into a barn like area where wood and all kinds of things were piled up. We passed an alcove from which a very pungent odour assailed the nostrils. Passing quickly on through another door we entered the dim interior of the single living room. In one corner stood an ancient iron bedstead covered with patchwork quilts. A little girl of about twelve was sitting on the bed, two cats rolled around the floor and two aged ladies sat on hard wooden chairs. One lady had a constant drop of water suspended at the end of her rather long nose. Both of these old ladies had woolly scarfs wrapped around their heads while on their feet they had knee length felt boots. On the table lay the black iron frying pan containing the remains of the last meal congealing in the fat. With typical Russian hospitality they offered us a meal from the frying pan which I declined with a little too much haste. Next we were offered tea. There was to be no way out for me, tea we would have to drink! The cold strong tea was poured into the cups and the hot water was added. My cup was blue and white with streaks of tea left by the previous drinker still visible to testify that the cups had not been washed in between. The rim was so well chipped that it was impossible to find a smooth place to drink from. I did not feel much like drinking the tea but down it had to go. As we were drinking our tea my friend was speaking to the ladies in Russian and what he said caused a minor commotion. One lady gestured towards me with the packet of tea and I could see 'Spar Premium Tea Bags' printed in English on the packet! The other old lady fell down on her knees and seized my hand and pressed it repeatedly to her lips while calling me her son and pronouncing many blessings on me. What had my friend said to provoke such a stir? He had told them that I was from The Eschol Trust and they were so happy to meet me. The tea and the tinned food in the little house had come from Northern Ireland.

The ambulance had problems in getting to Evjalova, the waggon for the corpse had problems getting to Evjalova, the mains water had not yet reached Evjalova but cans of food bearing the John 3:16 labels had managed to get to this neglected village to tell some of its isolated inhabitants the message of God's love. The military base is almost deserted with most of it's soldiers gone but the Lord's little 'Tin Soldiers' are marching on to conquer hearts and lives in Russia.

CHAPTER FIFTEEN

Christmas Cafe

Christmas is always a special time for us when we try to send extra gifts of food to the people. I never seem to have time for Christmas shopping or special activities in the time leading up to Christmas. It seems to me that it is really the time for serving others and demonstrating God's love rather than a time for indulgence and over eating. What better way to celebrate Christ's birth than to do something for those in real need of His love. For several years we organised lorry loads of frozen chickens which were distributed to the people in St. Petersburg after the Christmas morning service at the church. Russians celebrate Christmas on January 7 so it is possible for me to be at home with the family on December 25 and still reach Russia with help in time to make Christmas special for a lot of people there.

I remember the first time we tried to take a fridge full of chickens. There were all sorts of difficulties to overcome and it was only at the very last moment that we managed to get clearance from the veterinary officer at Dundonald House to export the chickens. It was December 29 when we got the approval. There was a big rush to get to O'Kanes and load the chickens on to our fridge. We were still short of some vital paper work and Mr. O'Kane thought we would not succeed. He was surprised when the Lord answered our prayers and acknowledged that it was only the Lord who could get us through. Well the Lord did really get us through and we distributed the chickens in St. Petersburg.

There was still one problem concerning the chickens, we had absolutely no funds towards paying for them. No one knew anything about our taking the chickens for everything happened at the last moment. We could not really expect anyone to send a gift towards the purchase of chickens if they did not know about. Could we? I came back to England from Russia and as soon as I left the ship I called to Pat to ask about everything. I remember asking her if any thing had been given towards the chickens and she told me that not one penny had been given since I left for Russia., I was praying as I drove through England because I would need to pay Mr. O'Kane very soon. It was just a few days later that the phone rang and a person who was a stranger to me asked about our work. The caller was ringing from England and they asked quite a few questions. The person then said, "I suppose that it takes a lot of money to do all that work and you would be glad if someone gave you something for it?" I replied that at that moment I would be very glad if someone gave me five, I meant five pounds. A few days later that person sent a gift of five thousand pounds. It covered the cost of the chickens, the fridge lorry and the shipping. We were able to pay all the outstanding accounts because of that one gift. The Lord is surely no man's debtor. At the end of every project I always like to end up with nothing left. I don't think the Lord gives us funds to store up. The money given for His work should be used to get His work done. When there is a new need then we must trust Him again to meet it rather than drawing on some reserve fund. We have never had a surplus but we have always had just enough. Our only reserve is Faith in God.

For some years I was thinking about how we could do something more for the pensioners, invalids and needy poor at Christmas. Then the Lord put an idea into my heart and mind. We could run a kind of Christmas Cafe where people could come and get a free meal and some presents to take home. We could give them Gospel literature and share the Love of Jesus with them in a practical way. All we would need would be a place from which to operate and permission to do it. We could bring everything else from Northern Ireland that we would need to put on a great Christmas dinner for the people. It seemed like a good idea but when I tried to get the needed permission from the authorities it proved to be very difficult. It was something which had never been done in Russia before and there were all kinds of rules and regulations concerning foreigners working and preparing food. I tried to get permission in several places without success and then we went to Belarus for our summer camp.

While we were there I was able to give a lot of help to the Radiological Institute and several other hospitals as well as to help feed the hundreds of Belarussian children at the camp. This helped to make a connection with some officials in the city of Minsk and I spoke to them concerning my idea.

We decided to co-operate with the members of the Messianic Congregation in the city on this project and approached Dr. Mark Levin. Another local organisation with connections to all the old army veterans was also enlisted because I was thinking about those elderly former soldiers. Meetings were held with all these people to discuss the details and then I had to visit all the officials to seek permission. It is impossible here to write down all the details but the Lord went before us and prepared the way. One man whose permission was vital turned out to be the father of a girl who had been to Northern Ireland with the choir, he was so grateful for the help his daughter received that he was prepared to do all he could to help us.

One morning I had to go to the Supreme Soviet to make the final agreements. As I entered the building I noticed the hammer and sickle logo over the door. In the office there was a huge portrait of V. I.. Lenin on the wall and some fresh flowers had been placed on a shelf underneath. The official who came to speak with me about our project began to ask me lots of difficult questions. "How many people will you feed every day?" he asked.

I really had not thought about that, all I wanted was a place to which I could invite the people where we could give them something nice to eat and share with them the love of Christ. I thought about it for a moment and decided that if I was to suggest too low a number the official would think I was not serious. After a while I said, "Six hundred." Now he asked me, "For how many days do you want to operate this cafe?" I said that I thought it would be ten days and he immediately did a little bit of multiplication on his note pad. Then he looked at me and said, "So you agree to feed six thousand people?" I was startled at the thought of the enormity of it! I felt a lump in my throat as I gulped and said that was correct. He then began to ask me how we would manage it and where we would get the workers and how we would invite the people and from where we would get the food and all sorts of other questions. I really had not considered any of those questions and as I replied to each one in turn I said, "I don't know how it will work out because this is an experiment and I have never done it before."

Many times I told him that this was an experiment and I did not know all the answers. Eventually all the questions had been asked and answered at least in part, I must have been able to satisfy him for he granted us permission to begin the cafe on January 7 for ten days. We had found a suitable place called 'Cafe Nemiga' right in the centre of Minsk and I made the contract to rent the premises and pay for the heat and light. I agreed to hire the staff there to work with our team from Ireland so now everything was signed and sealed and I was committed.

I was staying that night in Minsk at the home of Ludmilla and Volodia who are dear friends of mine. Their apartment is small and when I stay there they have to make room for me on the sofa in the living room. Everyone went off to bed and I was sitting there thinking over all that had happened during the day and about all my commitments. As I thought about trying to feed six thousand human beings with Christmas dinners my faith began to fail me. I felt the burden grow so heavy and I was wavering.

I said to myself, "You have really done it this time, you have promised that you will feed six thousand people. What if you can not do it? What if the Lord does not answer? What if no one volunteers to come to work? What if you begin and after three days run out of food, the people will be standing there and you will have nothing to give them?" I was really worried at that moment and I did the only thing that you can do in such a moment, I turned to the Lord in prayer. After spending some minutes praying I picked up my Bible and asked the Lord if He had any word of encouragement to give me concerning this cafe, any word to lift up my heart at this moment of great need.

Very clearly the Lord turned me to Paul's second letter to the Corinthians and the ninth chapter. I began to read the verses and suddenly found the words in verse six. "He which soweth sparingly shall reap also sparingly; and he which soweth bountifully shall reap also bountifully." That really encouraged me, if you want a bountiful harvest then sow bountifully. As I read on down though the verses I came to verse thirteen, "Whiles by the experiment of this ministration they glorify God for your professed subjection to the Gospel of Christ, and for your liberal distribution unto them and unto all men." That morning in the office when I was asked all the questions I had told the official that this was an experiment. I really did not know that the word experiment was in the Bible but here it was right on the page and the Lord just gave it back to me at the right moment. This 'experiment' was going to glorify the Lord so He must be going to supply all we needed for it to be a success. There was going to be a "liberal distribution unto them and unto all men." To those who came to the cafe and to others who could not come, to Jews and to Gentiles. With such a word of encouragement how could I doubt any longer? How could I feel anxious for a moment more? I simply read the last verse, "Thanks be unto God for His unspeakable gift." and then I thanked the Lord and went off to sleep. Early the next morning I went to the airport and then on to the flight for London and eventually arrived in Aldergrove. Pat met me at the airport as usual and I told her, "We have been given the green light to go ahead with the cafe, we are going to try to feed six thousand people." My poor wife who worries about all these things began at once to ask how I would manage it, where would I get all the food. I thought I was back in the office at Minsk again with all her questions. I remember saying to her, "Pat don't worry, the Lord still owns the cattle on a thousand hills, maybe He will slaughter one or two of them for us." I said it as a kind of half humorous remark. The Lord really did move to supply all the food that we needed and He sent all the personnel to work in the cafe too.

I was planning to take one lorry to Minsk to supply the cafe but actually we had to take four lorries loaded with food. The fishermen in Co. Donegal donated five tonnes of frozen fish for us to take to the cafe. This was a great gift because the Russian people are very fond of fish. From O'Kanes Poultry Ltd. I purchased another five thousand frozen chickens. The Lord began to send us amazing supplies from all over the place. One evening I was speaking at a meeting and as the people left the hall a man approached me and offered to donate potatoes for the cafe. I was grateful for his kind offer but I felt I had to refuse.

The reason being that we would be travelling during the worst of the winter and temperatures were expected to be low. The severe frost is always a problem in the winter and without protection even tins and bottles burst. It seemed a pity to refuse but the frost would only destroy the potatoes and they would be lost. It was exactly a week later as I was driving home from another meeting that I was praying to the Lord. I very often talk to the Lord as I drive along and bring all my thoughts to Him. I was telling the Lord how sorry I was that I could not bring the potatoes from Northern Ireland and wondering where in Minsk I was going to find good potatoes. Then the Lord spoke to me and He told me what to do, it was not an audible voice but He spoke in my heart. The Lord instructed me to make a big box out of polystyrene in the back of the trailer, the potatoes were to be put in the box and that would save them from the frost. Early next morning I opened up the hall at Loanends where we continued with the work of packing up the trailers. After some time I prepared to leave my friends there to carry on with the work while I went in search of polystyrene. I was just about to get into our van to drive off when a car arrived at the hall. It was a neighbour of mine who lived close by who had decided to donate to us the best lamb he had for the cafe. He was calling to ask about how to proceed with the butchering of the lamb. As he saw me about to enter the van he said, "Mr. McCracken are you going away somewhere?" I began to explain to him what I had in mind about the potatoes and he said that he felt it was a good solution to the problem. Then he said to me, "This is what you will do, you will go right now to the village of Doagh to a company called Springvale Poly Products Ltd. there you will ask for a man who is my cousin. Tell him what you need and he will work it all out for you, and tell him not to be too hard on you when it comes to paying the bill." It was not very long before I was at the factory where I spoke to the man on the internal telephone. My van was filled with twenty five big sheets of thick polystyrene and when I asked for the bill I was told to get on my way. When I said that I would have to pay for the polystyrene slabs first I was told that they were being donated free of charge because of the work we were doing.

I was thrilled by what the Lord had done in supplying the fish and the chickens and all else but somehow it seemed so wonderful that He had taken care about the polystyrene too. We constructed the big box and put several tonnes of potatoes into it and waited to see if it was really going to work. The potatoes arrived in Minsk in prime condition even though it was bitter winter weather. The polystyrene box worked perfectly. When all was loaded on to the four lorries we set off on the long drive to Belarus.

Our journey took us through Germany and Poland where we encountered a short delay on the border. We passed historic cities like Berlin and Warsaw on our way to the border of Belarus at Brest. There was plenty of snow in the fields and it was very cold but the roads were clear and no snow was falling as we drove. Our journey to Minsk was surprisingly easy and we had everything prepared for the arrival of the team of workers the Lord had sent us. Eighteen people from Ireland had volunteered to come with us to help staff the cafe and I had employed twenty two local people to work in the kitchens and four interpreters to help us speak to the people. With five drivers and myself we made up a party of fifty people all together who were involved in the cafe project. I had arranged that we would open the cafe on the Russian Christmas day at around five in the evening. That morning the sky was grey and the snow was falling briskly, the thermometer outside the hotel read twenty five degrees below zero and the river was frozen solid. I started the lorry with some difficulty and drove to the cafe where I planned to do some final preparations. Although it was still only eight thirty am. there was already a long line of elderly people waiting outside the premises. My plans were hastily revised and we opened for the first group at ten am. They had their meal and by eleven am. we were ready for the next group and so it continued through the day, every hour another group until we finished at eight thirty pm. For the next ten days we worked constantly serving the pensioners and needy poor of the city. Everyone received a good dinner of four courses and everyone received a present to take home with them as they were leaving. Each person who came was given a copy of the Gospel of Mark in Russian on the way out. During those ten days we served seven thousand two hundred meals to the people who came. Many other meals were sent out to people who were unable to come to the cafe due to old age or sickness. Our supplies of food did not run out, there was enough and to spare and afterwards we distributed the surplus food to hospitals and orphanages. Some foodstuff was sent to Moscow and to Klin and we were able to send some to St. Petersburg to replenish our store there. There was a liberal distribution to those who came and to lots of others too. So many kind words were spoken that it would be impossible to record them, so many tears of gratitude were shed that they would make a lake.

One elderly lady was leaving the cafe and her parting words made it all seem worth while. This is what she said, "Now I know for the first time in my life that the name Jesus Christ is not just something written in a book, now I know that He is real."

On Friday night we put on a special Shabbat dinner for the Jewish people and it was a joy to see the cafe filled to overflowing. The children's choir came and sang the choruses they had been taught by us when they were in Ireland. As the Sabbath candles burned we had the privilege of sharing with them the good news that Messiah has already come. They enjoyed the traditional chicken noodle soup and the Gefilte fish which was followed by roast chicken and potatoes with all the trimmings.

At the close of the Sabbath evening just as the people were preparing to leave one old woman came to me and took my hand. This lady led me to the door of the cafe and as she stood there with tears streaming down her cheeks she began to tell me a sad story. During the war the Nazi forces invaded Minsk and collected all the Jews into a ghetto. The wire fence of the ghetto had been just across the street from the cafe where we now stood. Inside that ghetto conditions were terrible and people died from starvation. As the old woman told me her story she gestured across the street and said, "My brother and my sister fell down dead just there in the ghetto. Now after all these years you have come here to feed us and to tell us of the love of God." We were both shedding tears as she left with her arms full of presents that evening. The Cafe Nemiga project was a great deal of hard work, and the responsibility was very heavy. I was constantly praying to the Lord that He would preserve everyone from accidents in the kitchen. What if someone was scalded with boiling water? Then there were concerns about the 'customers' what if someone came to the cafe and afterwards became ill or even died? Even if we were not responsible some people would think that our food had poisoned them. Standards of hygiene had to be maintained daily and all our staff had to wear white coats and hats as they went about their work. One day the health inspectors came to check us out and I was so glad that every single one of our team was properly attired in their white clothes and hats. The inspectors had a look around for a few minutes and then said, "Keep up the good work." The Lord watched over us all and the whole project passed off without any accident or incident to mar it. Every day the media carried stories about the cafe and it was tremendous to see newspapers which for years carried only Communist propaganda putting the story on the front page. When the cafe project was finished the team flew back to Aldergrove and I drove back home in the last lorry. I thought to myself, "Well, praise the Lord the vision has been accomplished, thousands have been blessed and now the cafe project is over."

The Lord had other plans though for a few weeks later I was in Klin not far from Moscow and the Mayor took me to see a cafe. The building was a bit dilapidated but there was a good kitchen and the oven worked although it was either full heat on or all off. Pavel made an appeal for me to help the pensioners and the invalids in Klin. He had heard about our project in Minsk and would like us to do the same in Klin we could have the place free of charge and give out all the Gospels we wanted to if we would only come.

So the idea for 'Cafe Tchaikovsky' was born in my heart and we found a team of twenty five workers who came to Klin to serve eight thousand meals to the needy there. Once again the Lord was gracious to us and provided all we needed. Once again we filled four lorries with supplies of food and drove them out through the snow. We checked with the Russian authorities before leaving and we were told that there would be no problem at the border with frozen chicken as long as we had the proper documents. We were told that we must not bring smoked or cooked chicken. Imagine our surprise then on our arrival at the border when we were told that it was possible only to bring smoked or cooked chicken but absolutely impossible to bring frozen chickens. This was exactly the opposite to the information we had been given a week before. It took three days of hard struggle and a lot of prayers before we managed to get the chickens through that border. I had to leave two lorries behind and go to Klin with the other two so as to be able to exert some pressure on the authorities. In the end we won the victory and got everything through. The delay put us under a great deal of extra pressure and meant the drivers and I had to work all through the night to be ready in time. It was difficult but with the help of the Lord we made it. Once again we started on the Russian Christmas day and through our service demonstrated in a practical way that Christ's coming was not just a story but a reality.

During the time we were loading the lorries at Loanends in preparation for our departure I remembered that in Minsk the old people had encountered some problems carrying home their presents. Tins of food tended to get dropped in the snow by arthritic fingers numbed from the cold. People often sent us some tins in a polythene bag and I decided we should keep them carefully and use them to give the people their presents in a convenient way. One day as I was sorting and folding bags at Loanends I noticed that almost every bag had a name printed on it advertising the shop from which it had come. I suddenly thought that we should be doing the same thing.

I rushed home and began to telephone all the polythene bag manufacturers listed in the yellow pages. It was two weeks before Christmas and everybody was wanting to get finished with their orders, no one wanted to take on new work. Then I spoke to Mr. Angus Brow of Brow Packaging in East Belfast and he invited me to drop in 'some day' to discuss my idea. 'Some day' was that very day! I was at the office within an hour and we discussed the things I had in mind. Mr. Brow pulled out all the stops at his plant and made us a strong polythene bag and printed on it in Russian the words, "Jesus is the best gift." and "For God so loved the world that He gave His only begotten Son that whosoever believeth on Him should not perish but have everlasting life." The bags also had the same details as the labels on our tins so that interested people could write to us for more information. Brow Packaging managed to supply us with thousands of these polythene carrier bags in time for Christmas and we took them to Cafe Tchaikovsky where every person received a bag full of good things to take home. The Lord blessed the Cafe Tchaikovsky project to thousands of really needy people and it was a special thrill to see hundreds of people walking in the town street carrying their bags which said, "Jesus is the best gift." A few years ago it would have been impossible to think of such a thing. Gordon Peters and I could never have imagined back in 1974 that a day would come when hundreds of thousands of Russian Jews would be in Israel. We could not have dreamed that it would one day be possible to bring children from Russia to teach them about Jesus. All of this was beyond even our imagination but it was not beyond the ability of the Lord to make it happen.

One night during a time when we were packing trailers I was working very late at Loanends after all the helpers had gone home to bed. I was trudging backwards and forwards carrying boxes in my blistered hands. I was tired and footsore from walking backward and forwards all day to the trailer with the heavy boxes. Maybe I was feeling a little bit lonely and sorry for myself and I complained to the Lord about the lack of dedicated helpers. I said to Him, "Lord here I am working like a donkey and you called me to be a preacher, what am I doing here in the middle of the night?" Then the Lord spoke to me in reply. "Once I needed a little donkey to carry me down the Mount of Olives in Jerusalem. That little unbroken colt had to bear the burden or I could not have received my triumph and my Glory as I entered Jerusalem that day. Sometimes I need donkeys to do my work. So just carry on being a donkey for me." I returned to the work with a lighter step and a praising heart. The boxes no longer seemed so heavy or my feet so sore.

If carrying these boxes would bring Him glory then I would just carry on until He would say enough. He has not said it yet. He is still saying to me, "Withdraw not thine hand" so I know that He will supply all we need in answer to our prayers and that His Ravens will still fly.

This is neither all of the story or the end of it. But it is the end of this book. I have written it that the Lord might be glorified and receive the praise for all that He has done. To us has been given the unspeakable privilege to share in His work. It is His work not ours.

About the Author

Ronnie McCracken was born in the tough Tiger's Bay area of North Belfast where he spent most of his early years. He was educated at the well known Currie Junior school and Mountcollyer Secondary. Ronnie says that the thing he liked best about school was the bell that signalled the end of the day. While still a teenager he came under the influence of the Gospel through a friend and decided to follow Jesus. This decision marked a dramatic change in his life. Ronnie studied for two years at night classes organised by the Belfast Bible College and then became a full time student of theology in Manchester. During the time he was a student he was a also a pastor of a small fellowship in Blackpool. Ronnie says that those days in Blackpool were among the happiest of his life. He was also involved in pastoral ministry in Northern Ireland and for several years he was an evangelist with the Irish Alliance of Christian Workers Unions. Ronnie McCracken has had a lifetime interest in the Jewish people and has organised more than fifty Holy Land tours over the years. Fifteen years ago he became the full time representative in Ireland of The Messianic Testimony, a mission founded by David Baron who was himself a Russian Jew. Ronnie has written the life story of David Baron under the title 'A Prince in Israel' which has appeared in both English and Russian. His interest in Russia and China has been consistent through many years, He was arrested in Russia in 1974 for 'smuggling' Bibles and for several years was forbidden to return. That changed when Gorbachev brought in his reforms.

The Eschol Trust

Ronnie's ministry has supported the Trust from its inception as a private fund in the seventies. It is now a registered charity. The Eschol Trust is dedicated to sending humanitarian help to the countries of the former Soviet Union as a means of sharing the Gospel. No one is employed by the Trust, all helpers are volunteers who work without payment. People often ask the question, "Why Eschol?" When Moses sent out his spies to view the Promised Land two came back with a good report. To show how good the land was they brought back a huge bunch of grapes. They cut the grapes in the valley of Eschol not far from Bethlehem. Just as they carried something to show the possibilities open to men of faith so Eschol Trust seek to carry the good and sweet things to show the love of the Lord.

To emphasise that the Eschol Trust is a locally based charity a slightly different spelling from that found in the Bible is used for the official name.

The Trust will be glad to hear from interested friends or helpers and can be contacted about the work at

241 Seven Mile Straight,
Crumlin, BT29 4YT
or PO Box 5 Crumlin.
Tel: 01232 825419 • Fax: 01232 825246

The proceeds from the sale of this book will be used for the benefit of the children of the Republic of Belarus who have suffered so much from the Chernobyl fallout.